中学生短期汉语教程

嘿！汉语

课本（上）

主　编　马燕华

编　者　伏学凤　胡秀梅　李晟宇
　　　　汝淑媛　汪　琦　杨　泉
　　　　（以姓氏音序排列）

北京语言大学出版社
BEIJING LANGUAGE AND CULTURE
UNIVERSITY PRESS

© 2019 北京语言大学出版社，社图号 18183

图书在版编目（CIP）数据

嘿！汉语．课本．上 ／ 马燕华主编；伏学凤等编写．－－ 北京：北京语言大学出版社，2019.6
（汉语纵横）
中学生短期汉语教程
ISBN 978-7-5619-5336-5

Ⅰ．①嘿… Ⅱ．①马… ②伏… Ⅲ．①汉语－对外汉语教学－教材 Ⅳ．① H195.4

中国版本图书馆 CIP 数据核字（2018）第 258266 号

嘿！汉语　课本（上）
HEI! HANYU　KEBEN (SHANG)

英文翻译：	孙齐圣　Ferlyn Wong Wai Kuan
英文编辑：	侯晓娟
插图绘制：	冰河插画
排版制作：	北京创艺涵文化发展有限公司
责任印制：	周　燚

出版发行：	北京语言大学出版社
社　　址：	北京市海淀区学院路 15 号，100083
网　　址：	www.blcup.com
电子信箱：	service@blcup.com
电　　话：	编 辑 部　8610-82303647/3592/3395
	国内发行　8610-82303650/3591/3648
	海外发行　8610-82303365/3080/3668
	北语书店　8610-82303653
	网购咨询　8610-82303908
印　　刷：	北京虎彩文化传播有限公司

版　次：	2019 年 6 月第 1 版	**印　次：**	2019 年 6 月第 1 次印刷
开　本：	889 毫米 × 1194 毫米　1/16	**印　张：**	8
字　数：	136 千字	**定　价：**	68.00 元

PRINTED IN CHINA

前 言

随着汉语作为外语教学的普及，学习汉语的外国人在年龄、母语、地域、职业、需求以及文化背景诸方面都呈现出越来越多的个体特色。一套教材"独领风骚"的局面已被万种教材相互竞争所替代。面对汉语教材"万花争艳"的形势，新教材必须具有"独秀之处"，必须特色鲜明。

《嘿！汉语》是为短期修学来华学习汉语的外国中学生编写的入门教材。它有四点鲜明特色。

一 为同一篇课文，编写多种技能练习。

外国中学生短期修学来华学习汉语的特点是：时间短，起点低，课程少。

为了适合短期修学汉语教学需要，本教材从零起点开始。为了能在一门课里同时训练听、说、读、写、译单项技能，我们为每篇课文编写了听力、会话、句法、阅读、写作、翻译单项技能练习，既满足了"一门课一本书"的短期教学需要，又达到了听、说、读、写、译单项技能的全面训练。

二 突出交际功能，取消语言点注释。

短期修学来华学习汉语，重在培养兴趣、获得成就感。本教材以语言交际最基本功能为纲编写课文，每课均提示本课主要交际功能及典型例句。同时取消了"语言点注释"，尝试从交际功能角度解释语言点，或许能减轻初级汉语语言点解释的学究气，突出短期学习汉语的体验性和实用性。

三 划分词语学习层次，提高词语复现率。

本教材从以下三方面控制难度。一是划分词语学习层次。"生词"是要求学生掌握的词语，尽可能列出扩展短语，尝试将双音节词中的自由语素拆分后分别解释意义；"补充词语"是备用的相关词语，减少了每课生词学习量。二是练习中复现学过的词语。每课练习题千方百计复现学过的词语，做到不出现生词。采取"滚雪球"方式将学过的词语"滚进来"编成较长语篇，让学生做阅读理解练习。这样不仅大大提高了生词复现率，而且使前后课文衔接更为紧密。三是充分利用英语和拼音来降低难度。每段课文下面均有英语翻译，同时做到凡是要学生"做"的地方，一定有英语翻译，凡是有汉字的地方，一定有汉语拼音。

四 增加"玩儿"的内容。

为适应中学生学习特点，本教材为每课学习内容设计了操作性强的课堂游戏，提供了较为丰富的中国人耳熟能详的古诗、童谣、绕口令和中文歌曲。

  本教材包括课本（上册、下册）、练习册（上册、下册），每册练习册中含三份单元测试卷和一份总测试卷。

  感谢伏学凤、胡秀梅为本教材试用版所做的大量认真而细致的编辑工作。

  感谢我院留学生 Vincent Richer 和 Kristie Xian 前期的英语翻译工作。

  北京语言大学出版社以出版对外汉语教材而享誉全球，相信《嘿！汉语》在北京语言大学出版社打造下能得到更多人的使用和喜爱。

马燕华
2018 年夏

Preface

With the popularity of teaching Chinese as a foreign language, foreign students are more and more characterized by different ages, native languages, regions, occupations, needs, and cultural backgrounds. The era of a set of good-for-all teaching materials has been taken over by that of tens of thousands of choices of textbooks. In such a fierce competition, new teaching materials must be unique with distinctive features.

Hi! Chinese is designed for middle school foreign beginners in China for a short-term Chinese study. It has the following four distinctive features:

 Providing exercises to develop multiple skills in each lesson

Programs for short-term middle school foreign students studying in China are usually short, at entry level, and with limited curriculum.

To meet the needs for short-term Chinese study, this textbook starts from the basics of Chinese learning. Listening, conversation, syntax, reading, writing, and translation practices are included in each lesson to train the skills in listening, speaking, reading, writing, and translation. It not only satisfies the needs of "a book for a course" in short-term study, but also helps to train all of the skills above.

 Highlighting communicative functions and removing notes on language points

A short-term program emphasizes cultivating students' interest and their obtaining a sense of achievement. This textbook is written based on the most essential functions in language communication, with each lesson beginning with the main communicative functions and typical examples. At the same time, the "notes on language points" have been removed and the language is explained from the perspective of communicative functions. It may make basic Chinese grammar learning less academic, but more practical in short-term study.

 Hierarchical vocabulary learning and increased recurrence rate of words

The textbook determines the degree of difficulty from the following three aspects. First, vocabulary learning is divided into different levels. "New words" are what students are required to master. The extended phrases are listed whenever possible and the free morphemes in two-syllable words are explained separately. "Supplementary words" include alternate related words, which reduces the amount of learning of each lesson.

Second, the words that have been learned are reviewed in practice. In practices of each lesson, these words reappear in various ways so that there won't be new words. The learned words are edited into longer texts as reading comprehension exercises like a snowball, thus greatly increasing the recurrence rate of new words and guaranteeing the continuity of the whole text. Third, English and *pinyin* are used to reduce the difficulty. There is English translation under each paragraph so that students have English translation wherever they need. Wherever there are Chinese characters, there must be *pinyin*.

 ## 4 More fun games and activities

In order to suit the learning characteristics of middle school students, the textbook has practical class games for each lesson, as well as abundant ancient Chinese poems, nursery rhymes, tongue twisters and Chinese songs which are familiar to Chinese people.

Hi! Chinese includes textbooks (volume 1 and volume 2), and workbooks (volume 1 and volume 2). Each volume of workbook is composed of three unit tests and one final test.

I would like to thank Fu Xuefeng and Hu Xiumei for their large amount of diligent and meticulous work in the edition of the trial version.

Thanks also go to Vincent Richer and Kristie Xian, international students of College of Chinese Language and Culture, Beijing Normal University, for their participation in the early English translation work.

Beijing Language and Culture University Press is known globally as a leader in publishing textbooks of teaching Chinese as a foreign language. I believe that, with its efforts, *Hi! Chinese* will be used and loved by more people.

Ma Yanhua
Summer 2018

使用说明

一、每课用 4 课时完成。

第 1、2 课时讲解生词，分析课文主要功能句，做练习册中对应的第二部分口语练习、第三部分句法阅读练习。

第 3、4 课时，可先用师生提问形式复习本课主要功能句，然后做练习册中对应的第一部分听力练习，最后开展第五部分游戏与活动。

二、每周学习 5 课，周五可抽出一节课做练习册中的单元测试，作为对平时学习情况的检查。

三、如果学习对象汉语水平非零起点，可先用练习册（上）中的总测试卷进行成绩测试。60 分以上者，可从下册开始学习；60 分以下者，应学习上册，进度可适当加快。

四、本教材上、下册标准教学时间均为三周，教材使用者亦可根据所教班级的教学时间加以调整，以适应一周班、两周班教学需要。

马燕华

2018 年 8 月

汉语拼音声母表

b	p	m	f	d	t	n	l
g	k	h		j	q	x	
zh	ch	sh	r	z	c	s	

汉语拼音韵母表

	i	u	ü
a	ia	ua	
o		uo	
e	ie		üe
ai		uai	
ei		uei	
ao	iao		
ou	iou		
an	ian	uan	üan
en	in	uen	ün
ang	iang	uang	
eng	ing	ueng	
ong			iong

目 录
Contents

课号	标题	交际功能	重点词语	页码
1	你好	1. 见面打招呼：你好！ 2. 询问姓名：你叫什么名字？ 3. 告别：再见！	什么	1
2	我是美国人	1. 询问国籍：你是哪国人？ 2. 纠正信息：不，我不是韩国人，我是日本人。 3. 询问身份：你是中学生吗？ 4. 确认信息：是的，我是中学生。 5. 表达相同：你也是中学生吗？（我也是中学生。） 6. 询问第三者身份：她是谁？	哪、也、谁	6
3	我家有四口人	1. 询问家庭人口：你家有几口人？ 2. 介绍家庭成员数量：我家有四口人。 3. 表达有某类家庭成员：我有姐姐。 4. 表达没有某类家庭成员：我没有妹妹。 5. 询问对方相同问题的简略形式：你家呢？ 6. 称呼家庭成员：爸爸、妈妈、哥哥、姐姐、弟弟、妹妹 7. 称说数字 1—10	几、有、没有	12
4	教室在这儿	1. 询问处所：请问，卫生间在哪儿？ 2. 询问用汉语怎么称说某物："toilet"汉语怎么说？ 3. 表达感谢：谢谢。 4. 回复感谢：不客气。 5. 询问词语的意思："卫生间"是什么意思？	哪儿、怎么说	18
5	现在七点半	1. 询问时间：现在几点？ 2. 询问什么时间做什么事：你几点吃午饭？ 3. 表达什么时间做什么事：我十二点吃午饭。 4. 称说一天主要时间段：早上、上午、中午、下午、晚上 5. 钟点的读法	起床、上课、吃、午饭、睡觉	24

课号	标题	交际功能	重点词语	页码
6	今天星期六	1. 询问星期几：今天星期几？ 2. 表达星期几：今天星期六。 3. 询问日期：今天几号？ 4. 表达日期：今天九号。 5. 询问生日：你的生日是几月几号？ 6. 表达生日：我的生日是七月四号。 7. 称说月、日、星期：一月一日星期一	星期、月、日、号	30
7	我喜欢玩儿电脑游戏	1. 询问爱好：你的爱好是什么？/ 你们有什么爱好？ 2. 表达爱好：我的爱好是打篮球。/ 我喜欢上网。/ 我爱玩儿电脑游戏。 3. 称说爱好：打篮球、听音乐、玩儿电脑游戏、看电影	爱好、喜欢	36
8	我今天不舒服	1. 询问是否不舒服：你怎么了？ 2. 述说身体不舒服：我不舒服。/ 我拉肚子。/ 我很累。 3. 表达情况发生了变化：她拉肚子了。 4. 表达不能做某事：她今天不能来上课。 5. 表达想做某事：我想睡觉。 6. 表达不想做某事：我不想上课。 7. 表示转述：她说她今天不能来上课。	拉肚子、能、想	41
9	我买苹果	1. 询问购物意愿：您买什么？ 2. 询问价钱：苹果怎么卖？/ 苹果多少钱一斤？ 3. 人民币的读法	要、一共、花、您、钱	47
10	这是包子	1. 询问事物名称：这是什么？/ 那是什么？ 2. 点菜：我要一个西红柿炒鸡蛋、一碗米饭、一瓶可乐。 3. 表达某种食物好吃：中国菜很好吃。	这、那	52

课号	标题	交际功能	重点词语	页码
11	你可以坐地铁去故宫	1. 问路：去地铁站怎么走？ 2. 指路：往前走。 3. 询问如何去某地：请问，我怎么去故宫？ 4. 表达去某地的方式：坐地铁去故宫 5. 表达动作发生得快、顺利，用时短：往前走五分钟就到了。 6. 表示条件许可做某事：你可以坐地铁去故宫。 7. 称说时段	可以、坐、就	57
12	今天天气不错	1. 谈论天气：今天天气不错，不冷也不热。/昨天太热了。 2. 询问天气情况：明天天气怎么样？ 3. 表达转述：听说明天会下雨。 4. 表达程度很高：昨天太热了。 5. "会"表示可能：明天会下雨。	怎么样、会	63
13	我喜欢白色	1. 询问喜欢的颜色：你喜欢什么颜色？ 2. 表达喜欢的颜色：我喜欢红色。 3. 选择提问：你喜欢红色还是喜欢绿色？ 4. 称说颜色	颜色、衬衫、牛仔裤、还是	69
14	我会说一点儿汉语	1. 询问会说何种语言：你会说汉语吗？ 2. 表达外语水平：我会说一点儿汉语。 3. 询问学习时间：你学了多长时间汉语了？ 4. 说明动作持续的时间：我学了半年汉语了。 5. 表达学习体会：我觉得汉语声调很难。 6. 表达称赞：你的汉语真不错。 7. 表达谦虚：哪里哪里，马马虎虎。 8. 加强语气：学习汉语挺有意思的。	一点儿、难、好听、好看、有意思	75
15	一路平安	1. 表达即将发生的动作：我今天晚上就要回国了。 2. 询问动作发生的时间：你什么时候回国？ 3. 提出建议并希望同意：请告诉我你的邮箱，好吗？ 4. 询问手机号码：你的手机号码是多少？ 5. 表达选择：我会给你发微信，或者发短信的。 6. 表达送行祝愿：一路平安。	邮箱、手机、微信、短信	82
	附录			88

Lesson	Title	Communicative functions	Key words	Page
1	Hello	1. To greet someone: 你好！ 2. To ask someone's name: 你叫什么名字？ 3. To say goodbye: 再见！	什么	1
2	I am American	1. To ask about someone's nationality: 你是哪国人？ 2. To correct the information: 不，我不是韩国人，我是日本人。 3. To ask about someone's identity: 你是中学生吗？ 4. To confirm the information: 是的，我是中学生。 5. To indicate similarity: 你也是中学生吗？（我也是中学生。） 6. To ask about the identity of a third person: 她是谁？	哪、也、谁	6
3	There are four people in my family	1. To ask about the number of family members: 你家有几口人？ 2. To introduce the number of family members: 我家有四口人。 3. To indicate having a certain family member: 我有姐姐。 4. To indicate not having a certain family member: 我没有妹妹。 5. The abbreviated form of asking the other person the same question: 你家呢？ 6. To address family members: 爸爸、妈妈、哥哥、姐姐、弟弟、妹妹 7. The expression of numbers 1-10	几、有、没有	12
4	The classroom is here	1. To ask about a location: 请问，卫生间在哪儿？ 2. To ask how to say something in Chinese: "toilet" 汉语怎么说？ 3. To express gratitude: 谢谢。 4. To respond to thanks: 不客气。 5. To ask about the meaning of a word: "卫生间"是什么意思？	哪儿、怎么说	18
5	It's 7:30 now	1. To ask about the time: 现在几点？ 2. To ask when an action will be done: 你几点吃午饭？ 3. To indicate when an action will be done: 我十二点吃午饭。 4. The expression of major periods of time in a day: 早上、上午、中午、下午、晚上 5. The way to read the time	起床、上课、吃、午饭、睡觉	24

XI

Lesson	Title	Communicative functions	Key words	Page
6	Today is Saturday	1. To ask about the day of a week: 今天星期几？ 2. To indicate the day of a week: 今天星期六。 3. To ask about the date: 今天几号？ 4. To indicate the date: 今天九号。 5. To ask about someone's birthday: 你的生日是几月几号？ 6. To indicate someone's birthday: 我的生日是七月四号。 7. The expression of month/date/week: 一月一日星期一	星期、月、日、号	30
7	I like playing computer games	1. To ask about someone's hobby: 你的爱好是什么？/ 你们有什么爱好？ 2. To indicate someone's hobby: 我的爱好是打篮球。/ 我喜欢上网。/ 我爱玩儿电脑游戏。 3. The expression of hobbies: 打篮球、听音乐、玩儿电脑游戏、看电影	爱好、喜欢	36
8	I'm not feeling well today	1. To ask if someone is not feeling well: 你怎么了？ 2. To describe physical discomfort: 我不舒服。/ 我拉肚子。/ 我很累。 3. To indicate a change of the condition: 她拉肚子了。 4. To indicate inability to do something: 她今天不能来上课。 5. To indicate inclination to do something: 我想睡觉。 6. To indicate disinclination to do something: 我不想上课。 7. To relate something as told by another: 她说她今天不能来上课。	拉肚子、能、想	41
9	I want to buy apples	1. To ask about someone's shopping intention: 您买什么？ 2. To ask about the price: 苹果怎么卖？/ 苹果多少钱一斤？ 3. The way to read RMB	要、一共、花、您、钱	47
10	These are steamed stuffed buns	1. To ask the name of something: 这是什么？/ 那是什么？ 2. To order food: 我要一个西红柿炒鸡蛋、一碗米饭、一瓶可乐。 3. To indicate some food is delicious: 中国菜很好吃。	这、那	52

Lesson	Title	Communicative functions	Key words	Page
11	You can take the subway to the Imperial Palace	1. To ask the way: 去地铁站怎么走？ 2. To show the way: 往前走。 3. To ask the way to somewhere: 请问，我怎么去故宫？ 4. To indicate how to go somewhere: 坐地铁去故宫 5. To indicate an action is quick and smooth: 向前走五分钟就到了。 6. To indicate someone can do something as the condition permits: 你可以坐地铁去故宫。 7. The expression of duration	可以、坐、就	57
12	The weather is good today	1. To talk about the weather: 今天天气不错，不冷也不热。/ 昨天太热了。 2. To ask about the weather: 明天天气怎么样？ 3. To relate something as told by another: 听说明天会下雨。 4. To indicate a high degree: 昨天太热了。 5. "会" indicating a possibility: 明天会下雨。	怎么样、会	63
13	I like white	1. To ask about the color someone likes: 你喜欢什么颜色？ 2. To indicate the color someone likes: 我喜欢红色。 3. Alternative questions: 你喜欢红色还是喜欢绿色？ 4. The expression of colors	颜色、衬衫、牛仔裤、还是	69
14	I can speak a little Chinese	1. To ask about someone's ability to speak a language: 你会说汉语吗？ 2. To indicate someone's foreign language proficiency: 我会说一点儿汉语。 3. To ask about someone's duration of study: 你学了多长时间汉语了？ 4. To indicate the duration of an action: 我学了半年汉语了。 5. To indicate someone's learning experience: 我觉得汉语声调很难。 6. To praise someone: 你的汉语真不错。 7. To show modesty: 哪里哪里，马马虎虎。 8. To emphasize the tone: 学习汉语挺有意思的。	一点儿、难、好听、好看、有意思	75

Lesson	Title	Communicative functions	Key words	Page
15	Have a safe journey	1. To indicate an upcoming action: 我今天晚上就要回国了。 2. To ask when an action will be taken: 你什么时候回国？ 3. To make a proposal and hope the other party to agree: 请告诉我你的邮箱，好吗？ 4. To ask for someone's mobile phone number: 你的手机号码是多少？ 5. To indicate the options: 我会给你发微信，或者发短信的。 6. To express one's wishes when seeing someone else off: 一路平安。	邮箱、手机、微信、短信	82
	Appendices			88

第一课 你好 Lesson 1 Hello

Dì-yī kè Nǐ hǎo

交际功能 Communicative functions

1. 见面打招呼 To greet someone：你好！
2. 询问姓名 To ask someone's name：你叫什么名字？
3. 告别 To say goodbye：再见！

课文 Text

(一) 01-1

Dàwèi: Nǐ hǎo!
大 卫：你好！

Quán Zhēn'ài: Nǐ hǎo!
全 真 爱：你好！

Dawei: Hello!

Quan Zhen'ai: Hello!

(二) 01-2

Dàwèi: Nǐ jiào shénme míngzi?
大 卫：你叫什么名字？

Quán Zhēn'ài: Wǒ jiào Quán Zhēn'ài.
全 真 爱：我叫全真爱。

Dawei: What is your name?

Quan Zhen'ai: My name is Quan Zhen'ai.

(三) 01-3

xuéshēngmen: Lǎoshī hǎo!
学 生 们：老师好！

Wáng lǎoshī: Nǐmen hǎo!
王 老 师：你们好！

Students: Hello, Miss Wang!

Miss Wang: Hello, everyone!

(四) 01-4

Dàwèi: Zàijiàn.
大 卫：再见。

Quán Zhēn'ài: Zàijiàn.
全 真爱：再见。

Dawei: Goodbye.

Quan Zhen'ai: Bye-bye.

(五) 01-5

Nǐmen hǎo! Wǒ jiào Dàwèi. Zàijiàn!
你们好！我叫大卫。再见！

Hello, everyone! My name is Dawei. Goodbye!

生词 New words

1	你	nǐ	pron.	you	
2	好	hǎo	adj.	good, fine	你好
3	叫	jiào	v.	to call, to be known as	
4	什么	shénme	pron.	what	叫什么
5	名字	míngzi	n.	name	什么名字 / 叫什么名字 / 你叫什么名字
	名	míng	n.	name	
	字	zì	n.	(Chinese) character	
6	我	wǒ	pron.	I, me	

7	老师	lǎoshī	n.	teacher	老师好 / 老师叫什么名字
8	你们	nǐmen	pron.	(*plural*) you	
	们	men	suf.	*indicating a plural form*	你们 / 我们 / 老师们
9	再见	zàijiàn	v.	goodbye, bye-bye	
	再	zài	adv.	again	
	见	jiàn	v.	to see	

习写字 Learn to write the characters

交际功能 Communicative functions

1. 见面打招呼 To greet someone

"你好!"打招呼。

"你好!" is used to greet someone.

2. 询问姓名 To ask someone's name

"你叫什么名字?"询问姓名。

"你叫什么名字?" is used to ask someone's name.

3. 告别 To say goodbye

"再见。"表达告别。

"再见。" is used to say goodbye.

补充词语 Supplementary words

1	早上好	zǎoshang hǎo	Good morning!
2	晚上好	wǎnshang hǎo	Good evening!

第二课 我是美国人
Dì-èr kè　Wǒ shì měiguórén
Lesson 2　I am American

交际功能 Communicative functions

1. 询问国籍 To ask about someone's nationality：你是哪国人？
2. 纠正信息 To correct the information：不，我不是韩国人，我是日本人。
3. 询问身份 To ask about someone's identity：你是中学生吗？
4. 确认信息 To confirm the information：是的，我是中学生。
5. 表达相同 To indicate similarity：你也是中学生吗？（我也是中学生。）
6. 询问第三者身份 To ask about the identity of a third person：她是谁？

我是美国人 2

课文 Text

（一） 02-1

Dàwèi: Nǐ hǎo! Wǒ shì měiguórén, nǐ shì nǎ guó rén?
大卫：你好！我是美国人，你是哪国人？

Hésài: Wǒ shì mòxīgērén.
何赛：我是墨西哥人。

Dawei: Hi! I'm American. What about you?

Hesai: I'm Mexican.

（二） 02-2

Quán Zhēn'ài: Nǐ shì hánguórén ma?
全真爱：你是韩国人吗？

Tiánzhōng: Bù, wǒ bú shì hánguórén, wǒ shì rìběnrén.
田中：不，我不是韩国人，我是日本人。

Quan Zhen'ai: Are you South Korean?

Tianzhong: No, I'm not South Korean. I'm Japanese.

（三） 02-3

Hésài: Nǐ shì zhōngxuéshēng ma?
何赛：你是中学生吗？

Tiánzhōng: Shì de, wǒ shì zhōngxuéshēng.
田中：是的，我是中学生。

Hésài: Nǐ yě shì zhōngxuéshēng ma?
何赛：你也是中学生吗？

Dàwèi: Bù, Wǒ shì dàxuéshēng.
大卫：不，我是大学生。

Hesai: Are you a middle school student?

Tianzhong: Yes, I am.

Hesai: Are you a middle school student, too?

Dawei: No, I'm a college student.

(四) 02-4

田中：她是谁？

全真爱：她是老师。

Tianzhong: Who is she?

Quan Zhen'ai: She is the teacher.

(五) 02-5

我叫何赛，我是墨西哥人我是中学生。

My name is Hesai. I'm Mexican, and I'm a middle school student.

生词 New words

1	是	shì	v.	to be	
2	美国人	měiguórén		American	
	美国	Měiguó	p.n.	the United States	美国人 / 美国老师
	人	rén	n.	person, people	
3	哪	nǎ	pron.	which	

我是美国人 2

4	国	guó	n.	nation, country	哪国 / 哪国人 / 是哪国人 / 老师是哪国人
5	墨西哥人	mòxīgērén		Mexican	
	墨西哥	Mòxīgē	p.n.	Mexico	墨西哥人 / 墨西哥老师
6	吗	ma	part.	used at the end of an interrogative sentence	你是美国人吗 / 你是老师吗
7	不	bù	adv.	no, not	不是美国人 / 不是大卫
8	韩国人	hánguórén		South Korean	我是韩国人
	韩国	Hánguó	p.n.	South Korea	
9	日本人	rìběnrén		Japanese	
	日本	Rìběn	p.n.	Japan	
10	中学生	zhōngxuéshēng	n.	middle school student	我是中学生 / 美国中学生 / 哪国中学生 / 你是哪国中学生
	中学	zhōngxué	n.	middle school	
	学生	xuéshēng	n.	student	
11	是的	shì de		yes	
12	也	yě	adv.	too, also	也是中学生 / 也是墨西哥人
13	大学生	dàxuéshēng	n.	college student	
	大学	dàxué	n.	college, university	
14	她	tā	pron.	she, her	她叫全真爱 / 她是中国人 / 她是学生 / 她不是老师
15	谁	shéi	pron.	who	你是谁 / 谁叫全真爱 / 谁是老师 / 谁是美国人

习写字 Learn to write the characters

shì

nǎ

国
guó

人
rén

中
zhōng
middle, center

ma

xué
to study, to learn

shēng

yě

bù

tā

shéi

交际功能 Communicative functions

1. 询问国籍 To ask about someone's nationality

"你是哪国人?" 询问国籍。

"你是哪国人?" is used to ask about someone's nationality.

2. 纠正信息 To correct the information

"不,我不是韩国人,我是日本人。" 纠正询问信息。

"不,我不是韩国人,我是日本人。" is used to correct the information.

3. 询问身份 To ask about someone's identity

"你是中学生吗?" 询问身份。

"你是中学生吗?" is used to ask about someone's identity.

4. 确认信息 To confirm the information

"是的,我是中学生。" 确认询问信息,也可以只回答"是的"。

"是的,我是中学生。" is used to confirm the information. The answer can simply be "是的".

5. 表达相同 To indicate similarity

"你也是中学生吗?"(我也是中学生。)"也"表示相同。

"也" in "你也是中学生吗?(我也是中学生。)" indicates similarity.

(1) 何赛是中学生,田中也是中学生。

(2) 大卫是美国人,她也是美国人。

6. 询问第三者身份 To ask about the identity of a third person

"她是谁?" 询问第三者的身份。

"她是谁?" is used to ask about the identity of a third person.

补充词语 Supplementary words

1	小学生	xiǎoxuéshēng	n.	elementary school student, pupil
2	法国	Fǎguó	p.n.	France
3	西班牙	Xībānyá	p.n.	Spain
4	英国	Yīngguó	p.n.	UK
5	中国	Zhōngguó	p.n.	China
6	俄罗斯	Éluósī	p.n.	Russia

第三课 我家有四口人
Dì-sān kè　Wǒ jiā yǒu sì kǒu rén
Lesson 3　There are four people in my family

交际功能 Communicative functions

1. 询问家庭人口 To ask about the number of family members：你家有几口人？
2. 介绍家庭成员数量 To introduce the number of family members：我家有四口人。
3. 表达有某类家庭成员 To indicate having a certain family member：我有姐姐。
4. 表达没有某类家庭成员 To indicate not having a certain family member：我没有妹妹。
5. 询问对方相同问题的简略形式 The abbreviated form of asking the other person the same question：你家呢？
6. 称呼家庭成员 To address family members：爸爸、妈妈、哥哥、姐姐、弟弟、妹妹
7. 称说数字 The expression of numbers：1—10

我家有四口人 3

课文 Text

(一) 03-1

大卫：Nǐ jiā yǒu jǐ kǒu rén?
你家有几口人？

田中：Wǒ jiā yǒu sì kǒu rén.
我家有四口人。

Dawei: How many people are there in your family?

Tianzhong: There are four people in my family.

(二) 03-2

全真爱：Nǐ yǒu mèimei ma?
你有妹妹吗？

大卫：Wǒ méiyǒu mèimei, wǒ yǒu yí gè jiějie.
我没有妹妹，我有一个姐姐。

Quan Zhen'ai: Do you have a younger sister?

Dawei: No, I don't. I have an elder sister.

(三) 03-3

全真爱：Wǒ jiā yǒu sì kǒu rén: bàba, māma, dìdi hé wǒ. Nǐ jiā ne?
我家有四口人：爸爸、妈妈、弟弟和我。你家呢？

何赛：Wǒ jiā yǒu wǔ kǒu rén: bàba, māma, liǎng gè gēge hé wǒ.
我家有五口人：爸爸、妈妈、两个哥哥和我。

Wǒ ài tāmen.
我爱他们。

Quan Zhen'ai: There are four people in my family: my father, my mother, my younger brother and I. What about your family?

Hesai: There are five people in my family: my father, my mother, my two elder brothers and I. I love them.

(四) 🔊 03-4

Wǒ shì rìběnrén, jiào Tiánzhōng Hézi. Wǒ jiā yǒu sì kǒu rén: bàba,
我是日本人，叫田中和子。我家有四口人：爸爸、
māma, gēge hé wǒ.
妈妈、哥哥和我。

I am Japanese. My name is Tianzhong Hezi. There are four people in my family: my father, my mother, my elder brother and I.

生词 New words

1	家	jiā	n.	family	我家 / 你家 / 她家 / 老师家
2	有	yǒu	v.	to have	我有哥哥
3	几	jǐ	pron.	how many	
4	口	kǒu	m.	*measure word for family members*	四口人 / 几口人 / 你家有几口人
5	四	sì	num.	four	
6	没有	méiyǒu	v.	to not have	没有妹妹 / 没有名字
	没	méi	v.	to not have	
7	妹妹	mèimei	n.	younger sister	我妹妹 / 她妹妹 / 我有妹妹 / 她也有妹妹
8	一	yī	num.	one	

我家有四口人 3

9	个	gè	m.	most commonly used esp. before nouns which do not have special measure words of their own	一个妹妹 / 四个中学生 / 一个人 / 几个人
10	姐姐	jiějie	n.	elder sister	我姐姐 / 姐姐的朋友
11	爸爸	bàba	n.	father	我爸爸 / 你爸爸 / 我爸爸是老师
12	妈妈	māma	n.	mother	我妈妈 / 我妈妈是中国人
13	弟弟	dìdi	n.	younger brother	我弟弟 / 一个弟弟
14	和	hé	conj.	and	我和你 / 爸爸和妈妈 / 中学生和大学生
15	呢	ne	part.	used at the end of an interrogative sentence	你呢 / 你家呢 / 你爸爸呢 / 你们呢
16	两	liǎng	num.	(usually used before measure words and before 半, 千, 万, and 亿) two	两个哥哥 / 两口人
17	哥哥	gēge	n.	elder brother	我哥哥 / 哥哥是中学生 / 她没有哥哥 / 哥哥和妹妹
18	爱	ài	v.	to love	我爱你 / 我也爱你 / 我爱爸爸、妈妈 / 我爱老师
19	他们	tāmen	pron.	they, them	他们是谁 / 他们是中学生 / 他们没有妹妹 / 我爱他们

习写字 Learn to write the characters

jiā

yǒu

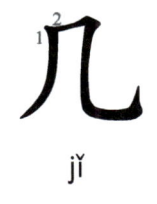
jǐ

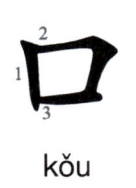
kǒu

bà
father

mā
mother

交际功能 Communicative functions

1. 询问家庭人口 To ask about the number of family members

"你家有几口人？"询问家庭人口。

"你家有几口人？" is used to ask about the number of family members.

2. 介绍家庭成员数量 To introduce the number of family members

"我家有四口人。"介绍家庭成员数量。

"我家有四口人。" is used to introduce the number of family members.

3. 表达有某类家庭成员 To indicate having a certain family member

"我有姐姐。"表达有某类家庭成员。

"我有姐姐。" is used to indicate having a certain family member.

4. 表达没有某类家庭成员 To indicate not having a certain family member

"我没有妹妹。"表达没有某类家庭成员。

"我没有妹妹。" is used to indicate not having a certain family member.

5. 询问对方相同问题的简略形式 The abbreviated form of asking the other person the same question

"名词 + 呢？"是询问对话中相同问题的简略形式。如，"我家有四口人，你家呢？"，意思是"你家有几口人？"

"我有姐姐，你呢？"，"你呢？"意思是"你有姐姐吗？"

"我是美国人，你呢？"，"你呢？"意思是"你是哪国人？"

"noun + 呢？" is the abbreviated form to ask the same question in a dialogue. For example, "我家有四口人，你家呢？" means "你家有几口人？".

In "我有姐姐，你呢？", "你呢？" is used to ask "你有姐姐吗？".

In "我是美国人，你呢？", "你呢？" is used to ask "你是哪国人？".

6. 称呼家庭成员 To address family members

"爸爸、妈妈、哥哥、姐姐、弟弟、妹妹"用于称呼家庭成员。

"爸爸"，"妈妈"，"哥哥"，"姐姐"，"弟弟" and "妹妹" are used to address family members.

7. 称说数字 1—10 The expression of numbers 1-10

"一、二、三、四、五、六、七、八、九、十"用于称说数字1—10。量词前的"二"，一般读作"两"，如"两口人"。

"一"，"二"，"三"，"四"，"五"，"六"，"七"，"八"，"九" and "十" are used to refer to numbers 1-10. When used before a measure word, "二" is usually read as "两", such as "两口人（liǎng kǒu rén）".

补充词语 Supplementary words

1	爷爷	yéye	n.	(paternal) grandpa
2	奶奶	nǎinai	n.	(paternal) grandma
3	外公	wàigōng	n.	(maternal) grandpa
4	外婆	wàipó	n.	(maternal) grandma
5	猫	māo	n.	cat
6	狗	gǒu	n.	dog

第四课　教室在这儿
Lesson 4　The classroom is here

交际功能 Communicative functions

1. 询问处所 To ask about a location：请问，卫生间在哪儿？
2. 询问用汉语怎么称说某物 To ask how to say something in Chinese："toilet"汉语怎么说？
3. 表达感谢 To express gratitude：谢谢。
4. 回复感谢 To respond to thanks：不客气。
5. 询问词语的意思 To ask about the meaning of a word："卫生间"是什么意思？

课文 Text

（一） 04-1

Dàwèi: Qǐngwèn, wèishēngjiān zài nǎr?
大卫：请问，卫生间在哪儿？

Hésài: Zài nàr.
何赛：在那儿。

Dàwèi: Jiàoshì ne?
大卫：教室呢？

Hésài: Zài zhèr.
何赛：在这儿。

Dawei: Excuse me, where is the toilet?

Hesai: Over there.

Dawei: Where is the classroom?

Hesai: Here it is.

（二） 04-2

Hésài: Lǎoshī, "toilet" Hànyǔ zěnme shuō?
何赛：老师，"toilet"汉语怎么说？

Wáng lǎoshī: Wèishēngjiān.
王老师：卫生间。

Hésài: Xièxie.
何赛：谢谢。

Wáng lǎoshī: Bú kèqi.
王老师：不客气。

Hesai: Miss Wang, how do you say "toilet" in Chinese?

Miss Wang: we say wèishēngjiān.

Hesai: Thank you.

Miss Wang: You're welcome.

(三) 04-3

Tiánzhōng: Lǎoshī, "wèishēngjiān" shì shénme yìsi?
田中：老师，"卫生间"是什么意思？

Wáng Lǎoshī: "Wèishēngjiān" yìsi shì "toilet".
王老师："卫生间"意思是"toilet"。

Tianzhong: Miss Wang, what is the meaning of wèishēngjiān?

Miss Wang: Wèishēngjiān means "toilet".

(四) 04-4

"toilet", Hànyǔ shuō "wèishēngjiān".
"toilet"，汉语说"卫生间"。

"Toilet" in Chinese is wèishēngjiān.

生词 New words

1	请问	qǐngwèn	v.	excuse me	
	请	qǐng	v.	please	
	问	wèn	v.	to ask	问老师 / 问爸爸
2	卫生间	wèishēngjiān	n.	toilet, restroom	
	卫生	wèishēng	n./adj.	hygiene; sanitary	
	间	jiān		room	
3	在	zài	v.	to be in/on/at	在家 / 在墨西哥

4	哪儿	nǎr	pron.	where	在哪儿 / 老师在哪儿
5	那儿	nàr	pron.	there	在那儿 / 老师在那儿
6	教室	jiàoshì	n.	classroom	在教室 / 一个教室
7	这儿	zhèr	pron.	here	在这儿 / 教室在这儿
8	汉语	Hànyǔ	p.n.	Chinese (language)	汉语老师 / 汉语名字
	汉	Hàn		Chinese	
	语	yǔ		language	
9	怎么	zěnme	pron.	how	
10	说	shuō	v.	to say	怎么说 / 说汉语 / 老师说
11	谢谢	xièxie	v.	to thank	谢谢你 / 谢谢老师 / 谢谢妈妈
12	不客气	bú kèqi		You are welcome.	
	客气	kèqi	adj./v.	polite	
13	意思	yìsi	n.	meaning	

习写字 Learn to write the characters

交际功能 Communicative functions

1. 询问处所 To ask about a location

"……＋在哪儿"询问处所。如,"请问,卫生间在哪儿?"

"……＋在哪儿" is used to ask about a location. For example: "请问,卫生间在哪儿?".

(1) 请问,教室在哪儿?

(2) 你家在哪儿?

2. 询问用汉语怎么称说某物 To ask how to say something in Chinese

"'toilet'汉语怎么说?"询问用汉语怎么称说某物。

"'toilet'汉语怎么说?" is used to ask how to say something in Chinese.

(1) "water"汉语怎么说?

(2) "Good morning!"汉语怎么说?

3. 表达感谢 To express gratitude

"谢谢。"表达感谢。

"谢谢。" is used to express gratitude.

4. 回复感谢 To respond to thanks

"不客气。"回复感谢。

"不客气。" is used to respond to thanks.

5. 询问词语的意思 To ask about the meaning of a word

"……是什么意思?"询问词语的意思。

"……是什么意思?" is used to ask about the meaning of a word.

(1) "卫生间"是什么意思?

(2) "早上好"是什么意思?

补充词语 Supplementary words

1	宿舍	sùshè	n.	dormitory
2	超市	chāoshì	n.	supermarket
3	读	dú	v.	to read
4	英语	Yīngyǔ	p.n.	English
5	西班牙语	Xībānyáyǔ	p.n.	Spanish
6	日语	Rìyǔ	p.n.	Japanese
7	韩语	Hányǔ	p.n.	Korean
8	法语	Fǎyǔ	p.n.	French
9	俄语	Éyǔ	p.n.	Russian

第五课 现在七点半
Dì-wǔ kè　Xiànzài qī diǎn bàn
Lesson 5 It's 7:30 now

交际功能 Communicative functions

1. 询问时间 To ask about the time：现在几点？
2. 询问什么时间做什么事 To ask when an action will be done：你几点吃午饭？
3. 表达什么时间做什么事 To indicate when an action will be done：我十二点吃午饭。
4. 称说一天主要时间段 The expression of major periods of time in a day：早上、上午、中午、下午、晚上
5. 钟点的读法
   The way to read the time

课文 Text

(一) 05-1

全真爱：现在几点？
Quán Zhēn'ài: Xiànzài jǐ diǎn?

田 中：现在七点半。
Tiánzhōng: Xiànzài qī diǎn bàn.

Quan Zhen'ai: What time is it now?

Tianzhong: It's 7:30.

(二) 05-2

全真爱：你几点吃午饭？
Quán Zhēn'ài: Nǐ jǐ diǎn chī wǔfàn?

田 中：我十二点吃午饭。
Tiánzhōng: Wǒ shí'èr diǎn chī wǔfàn.

Quan Zhen'ai: When are you going to have lunch?

Tianzhong: I'm going to have lunch at 12:00.

(三) 05-3

全真爱：你每天几点睡觉？
Quán Zhēn'ài: Nǐ měi tiān jǐ diǎn shuì jiào?

田 中：十一点。你呢？
Tiánzhōng: Shíyī diǎn. Nǐ ne?

全真爱：我每天十点半睡觉。
Quán Zhēn'ài: Wǒ měi tiān shí diǎn bàn shuì jiào.

Quan Zhen'ai: What time do you go to bed every night?

Tianzhong: 11:00 p.m.. How about you?

Quan Zhen'ai: I go to bed at 10:30 p.m. every night.

(四) 05-4

Wǒ měi tiān zǎoshang qī diǎn qǐ chuáng, qī diǎn bàn chī zǎofàn, shàngwǔ bā diǎn shàng kè,
我每天早上七点起床,七点半吃早饭,上午八点上课,
shíyī diǎn sìshí xià kè, zhōngwǔ shí'èr diǎn chī wǔfàn. Xiàwǔ méiyǒu kè. Wǎnshang
十一点四十下课,中午十二点吃午饭。下午没有课。晚上
liù diǎn bàn chī wǎnfàn, shíyī diǎn shuì jiào.
六点半吃晚饭,十一点睡觉。

I get up at 7:00 am and have breakfast at 7:30 a.m. every morning. The class begins at 8:00 a.m. and ends at 11:40 a.m.. I have lunch at 12:00. I don't have class in the afternoon. I have dinner at 6:30 p.m.. I go to sleep at 11:00 p.m..

生词 New words

1	现在	xiànzài	n.	now	
2	点	diǎn	m.	o'clock	几点 / 现在几点 / 八点 / 十二点
3	半	bàn	num.	half	七点半 / 八点半 / 十二点半
4	吃	chī	v.	to eat, to have	
5	午饭	wǔfàn	n.	lunch	吃午饭 / 不吃午饭 / 十二点吃午饭
	午	wǔ		noon	
	饭	fàn	n.	meal	吃饭 / 不吃饭
6	每天	měi tiān		every day	每天吃午饭 / 每天在家 / 每天说汉语
	每	měi	pron.	every	每人 / 每天
	天	tiān	m.	day	一天 / 两天 / 三天

现在七点半 5

7	睡觉	shuì jiào	v.	to sleep	十点半睡觉 / 不睡觉 / 在家睡觉
8	早上	zǎoshang	n.	morning	早上六点 / 早上起床 / 早上去
9	起床	qǐ chuáng	v.	to get up	六点起床 / 不起床 / 每天六点起床
	起	qǐ	v.	to rise to one's feet	
	床	chuáng	n.	bed	
10	早饭	zǎofàn	n.	breakfast	
11	上午	shàngwǔ	n.	morning	
12	上课	shàng kè	v.	to attend class	八点上课
	上	shàng	v.	to be engaged (in work, study, etc.) at a fixed time	
	课	kè	n.	class	
13	下课	xià kè	v.	to finish class	十二点下课 / 不下课
	下	xià	v.	to be off (work, school, etc.)	
14	中午	zhōngwǔ	n.	noon	
15	下午	xiàwǔ	n.	afternoon	下午没有课 / 下午六点 / 每天下午
16	晚上	wǎnshang	n.	evening, night	晚上十一点 / 每天晚上
17	晚饭	wǎnfàn	n.	dinner, supper	吃晚饭 / 不吃晚饭
	晚	wǎn	n.	evening; late	

习写字 Learn to write the characters

xiàn
now

diǎn

bàn

chī

wǔ

fàn

27

上 shàng

下 xià

课 kè

交际功能 Communicative functions

1. 询问时间 To ask about the time

"现在几点?"询问时间。

"现在几点?" is used to ask about the time.

2. 询问什么时间做什么事 To ask when an action will be done

"几点 + 动词短语"询问什么时间做什么事情。

"几点 + verb phrase" is used to ask when an action will be done.

（1）你几点吃晚饭?

（2）你几点起床?

3. 表达什么时间做什么事 To indicate when an action will be done

"时间 + 动词短语"表达什么时间做什么事情。如,"我十二点吃午饭。"

"Time + verb phrase" is used to indicate when an action will be done. For example: "我十二点吃午饭。".

（1）我早上六点起床。

（2）我们八点上课。

现在七点半 5

4. 称说一天主要时间段 The expression of major periods of time in a day

"早上、上午、中午、下午、晚上"用于称说一天主要时间段。

"早上","上午","中午","下午"and"晚上"are expressions of the major periods of time in a day.

5. 钟点的读法 The way to read the time

7:30 读作七点半

7:30 is read as qī diǎn bàn

8:00 读作八点

8:00 is read as bā diǎn

11:40 读作十一点四十

11:40 is read as shíyī diǎn sìshí

第六课 今天星期六

Dì-liù kè Jīntiān xīngqīliù

Lesson 6 Today is Saturday

交际功能 Communicative functions

1. 询问星期几 To ask about the day of a week：今天星期几？
2. 表达星期几 To indicate the day of a week：今天星期六。
3. 询问日期 To ask about the date：今天几号？
4. 表达日期 To indicate the date：今天九号。
5. 询问生日 To ask about someone's birthday：你的生日是几月几号？
6. 表达生日 To indicate someone's birthday：我的生日是七月四号。
7. 称说月、日、星期 The expression of month/date/week：一月一日星期一

今天星期六 6

课文 Text

(一) 🔊 06-1

Dàwèi: Jīntiān xīngqī jǐ?
大卫：今天星期几？

Tiánzhōng: Jīntiān xīngqīliù.
田中：今天星期六。

Dawei: What day is it today?

Tianzhong: Today is Saturday.

(二) 🔊 06-2

Tiánzhōng: Jīntiān jǐ hào?
田　中：今天几号？

Quán Zhēn'ài: Jīntiān jiǔ hào.
全真爱：今天九号。

Tianzhong: What date is it today?

Quan Zhen'ai: Today is 9th.

(三) 🔊 06-3

Hésài: Nǐ de shēngrì shì jǐ yuè jǐ hào?
何赛：你的生日是几月几号？

Dàwèi: Wǒ de shēngrì shì qī yuè sì hào.
大卫：我的生日是七月四号。

Hesai: When is your birthday?

Dawei: My birthday is on July 4th.

(四) 06-4

Jīntiān xīngqīliù, wǒmen méiyǒu kè, míngtiān xīngqītiān, wǒmen yě méiyǒu kè,
今天星期六，我们没有课，明天星期天，我们也没有课，

wǒ hěn gāoxìng. Zhōumò yúkuài!
我很高兴。周末愉快！

Today is Saturday. We don't have class. Tomorrow is Sunday. We also don't have class. I'm glad. Have a pleasant weekend!

生词 New words

1	今天	jīntiān	n.	today	今天星期六 / 今天上课 / 今天晚上
	今	jīn		present	
2	星期	xīngqī	n.	week	
3	星期六	xīngqīliù	n.	Saturday	星期六下午 / 星期六晚上
4	号	hào	m.	date	四号 / 五号 / 六号
5	的	de	part.	a particle indicating possession or modification	你的生日 / 我们的老师 / 我们的教室
6	生日	shēngrì	n.	birthday	妈妈的生日 / 妹妹的生日 / 哥哥的生日
	生	shēng	v.	to be born	
	日	rì		day	
7	月	yuè	n.	month	一月 / 二月 / 三月
8	明天	míngtiān	n.	tomorrow	
	明	míng		immediately following this year or this day, next	
9	星期天	xīngqītiān	n.	Sunday	
10	很	hěn	adv.	very	很好 / 很热 / 很冷

11	高兴	gāoxìng	adj.	glad, happy	很高兴 / 不高兴
12	周末	zhōumò	n.	weekend	
	周	zhōu	n.	week	周一 / 周六 / 周日
	末	mò	n.	end	
13	愉快	yúkuài	adj.	pleasant	很愉快 / 周末愉快

习写字 Learn to write the characters

jīn

tiān

xīng
star

qī
period

yuè

hào

míng

hěn

gāo
high

xìng
excitement

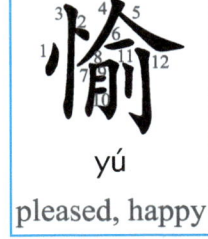
zhōu

mò

yú
pleased, happy

kuài
pleased, happy

交际功能 Communicative functions

1. 询问星期几 To ask about the day of a week

"……星期几?"询问星期几。如,"今天星期几?"

"……星期几?" is used to ask about the day of a week. For example: "今天星期几?".

2. 表达星期几 To indicate the day of a week

"星期~"表达星期几。如,"今天星期六。"

"星期一" is used to indicate the day of a week. For example: "今天星期六。".

3. 询问日期 To ask about the date

"……几号?"询问日期。

"……几号?" is used to ask about the date.

(1) 今天几号?

(2) 明天几号?

4. 表达日期 To indicate the date

"~号"表达日期。如,"今天九号。"

"~号" is used to indicate the date. For example: "今天九号。".

5. 询问生日 To ask about someone's birthday

"……生日是几月几号?"询问生日,如,"你的生日是几月几号?"

"……生日是几月几号?" is used to ask about someone's birthday. For example: "你的生日是几月几号?".

(1) 大卫的生日是几月几号?

(2) 全真爱的生日是几月几号?

询问生日一般只问哪月哪日,不问哪年。

Generally, only the month and the date instead of the year are asked when asking someone about his/her birthday.

另外,"的"放在被修饰限制的词语前面,表示前面的词语修饰、限制后面的词语。如,"你的生日、爸爸的生日、我们的教室","你、爸爸、我们"分别限制"生日、生日、教室"。

Besides that, if "的" is put before the word to be modified and restricted, it indicates that the word before "的" modifies and restricts the word after it. For example, in "你的生日", "爸爸的生日" and "我们的教室", "你", "爸爸" and "我们" restrict "生日", "生日", and "教室" respectively.

6. 表达生日 To indicate someone's birthday

"……生日是～月～号。"表达生日。如,"我的生日是七月四号。"

"……生日是～月～号。" is used to indicate someone's birthday. For example: "我的生日是七月四号。".

7. 称说月、日、星期 The expression of month/date/week

"号"与"日"都可以用来称说日期,口语常用"号"。

Both "号" and "日" can be used to express the date. "号" is more frequently used in spoken Chinese.

(1) 今天是七月四号。

(2) 她的生日是十二月二十五号。

"星期～",用来称说星期几。如,"星期一、星期二、星期三、星期四、星期五、星期六、星期天(日)"。

"星期～" is used to indicate the day of a week. For example: "星期一","星期二","星期三","星期四","星期五","星期六","星期天(日)".

称说的顺序是:月、号、星期。如"一月一号星期一"。

The order is "month", "date", and "day of a week". For example: "一月一号星期一".

第七课　我爱玩儿电脑游戏
Lesson 7　I like playing computer games

交际功能 Communicative functions

1. 询问爱好 To ask about someone's hobby：你的爱好是什么？/ 你们有什么爱好？
2. 表达爱好 To indicate someone's hobby：我的爱好是打篮球。/ 我喜欢上网。/ 我爱玩儿电脑游戏。
3. 称说爱好 The expression of hobbies：打篮球、听音乐、玩儿电脑游戏、看电影

7 我爱玩儿电脑游戏

课文 Text

(一) 🔊 07-1

何赛：你的爱好是什么？

大卫：我的爱好是打篮球。

Hesai: What is your hobby?

Dawei: My hobby is playing basketball.

(二) 🔊 07-2

王老师：你们有什么爱好？

田　中：我的爱好是听音乐。

全真爱：我喜欢上网。

何　赛：我爱玩儿电脑游戏。老师，你呢？

王老师：我喜欢看电影。

Miss Wang: What are your hobbies?

Tianzhong: My hobby is listening to music.

Quan Zhen'ai: I like surfing the Internet.

Hesai: I like playing computer games. What about you, Miss Wang?

Miss Wang: I like watching movies.

(三) 07-3

Wǒ shì Hésài, wǒ de àihào shì wánr diànnǎo yóuxì.
我是何赛，我的爱好是玩儿电脑游戏。

I'm Hesai, and my hobby is playing computer games.

生词 New words

1	爱好	àihào	n.	hobby	我的爱好 / 妈妈的爱好 / 爸爸的爱好
2	打	dǎ	v.	to play (ball games, etc.)	
3	篮球	lánqiú	n.	basketball	打篮球
	篮	lán	n.	basket	
	球	qiú	n.	ball	
4	听	tīng	v.	to listen, to hear	
5	音乐	yīnyuè	n.	music	听音乐 / 喜欢音乐 / 晚上听音乐
6	喜欢	xǐhuan	v.	to like	喜欢妈妈 / 喜欢中国 / 喜欢打篮球
7	上网	shàng wǎng	v.	to surf the Internet	喜欢上网 / 每天上网 / 每天晚上上网
	网	wǎng	n.	(the) Internet	
8	玩儿	wánr	v.	to play	
9	电脑	diànnǎo	n.	computer	我的电脑 / 他的电脑
10	游戏	yóuxì	n.	game	电脑游戏 / 玩儿游戏 / 打游戏
11	看	kàn	v.	to watch	
12	电影	diànyǐng	n.	movie	看电影

习写字 Learn to write the characters

 dǎ

 lán

 qiú

 xǐ to like

 huān joyous

 tīng

 kàn

 yīn sound

 yuè music

 wǎng

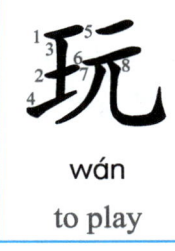 wán to play

 diàn electricity

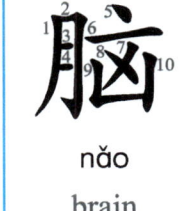 nǎo brain

 yǐng shadow

交际功能 Communicative functions

1. 询问爱好 To ask about someone's hobby

"你的爱好是什么?" 询问爱好。也可以说 "你有什么爱好?"

" 你的爱好是什么?" is used to ask about someone's hobby. You can also say " 你有什么爱好?".

2. 表达爱好 To indicate someone's hobby

"我的爱好是打篮球。"表达爱好，也可以说"我喜欢上网。""我爱玩儿电脑游戏。"

"我的爱好是打篮球。" is used to indicate someone's hobby. You can also say "我喜欢上网。" or "我爱玩儿电脑游戏。".

（1）她的爱好是听音乐。

（2）老师喜欢看电影。

（3）何赛爱玩儿电脑游戏。

3. 称说爱好 The expression of hobbies

一般用动词短语称说爱好。如，"打篮球、听音乐、玩儿电脑游戏、看电影"等。

Verb phrases are usually used to indicate someone's hobbies. For example: "打篮球","听音乐","玩儿电脑游戏","看电影", etc.

补充词语 Supplementary words

1	运动	yùndòng	v./n.	to do sports; sport
2	打太极拳	dǎ tàijíquán		to practice *taijiquan*
3	打网球	dǎ wǎngqiú		to play tennis
	网球	wǎngqiú	n.	tennis
4	踢足球	tī zúqiú		to play football
	足球	zúqiú	n.	football
	足	zú	n.	foot
5	打乒乓球	dǎ pīngpāngqiú		to play table tennis
	乒乓球	pīngpāngqiú	n.	table tennis
6	看书	kàn shū		to read a book
	书	shū	n.	book
7	看电视	kàn diànshì		to watch TV
	电视	diànshì	n.	TV
8	唱歌	chàng gē	v.	to sing

第八课　我今天不舒服
Dì-bā kè　Wǒ jīntiān bù shūfu
Lesson 8　I'm not feeling well today

交际功能 Communicative functions

1. 询问是否不舒服 To ask if someone is not feeling well：你怎么了？
2. 述说身体不舒服 To describe physical discomfort：我不舒服。/ 我拉肚子。/ 我很累。
3. 表达情况发生了变化 To indicate a change of the condition：她拉肚子了。
4. 表达不能做某事 To indicate inability to do something：她今天不能来上课。
5. 表达想做某事 To indicate inclination to do something：我想睡觉。
6. 表达不想做某事 To indicate disinclination to do something：我不想上课。
7. 表达转述 To relate something as told by another：她说她今天不能来上课。

41

课文 Text

(一) 08-1

Quán Zhēn'ài: Nǐ zěnme le?
全真爱：你怎么了？

Tiánzhōng: Wǒ dùzi téng.
田中：我肚子疼。

Quan Zhen'ai: What's the matter with you?

Tianzhong: My stomach hurts.

(二) 08-2

Quán Zhēn'ài: Lǎoshī, Tiánzhōng jīntiān bù shūfu.
全真爱：老师，田中今天不舒服。

Wáng lǎoshī: Tā zěnme le?
王老师：她怎么了？

Quán Zhēn'ài: Tā lā dùzi le. Tā shuō tā jīntiān bù néng lái shàng kè.
全真爱：她拉肚子了。她说她今天不能来上课。

Quan Zhen'ai: Miss Wang, Tianzhong is not feeling well today.

Miss Wang: What's wrong with her?

Quan Zhen'ai: She has diarrhea. She said that she could not attend class today.

(三) 08-3

Wáng lǎoshī: Hésài, nǐ yě bù shūfu ma?
王老师：何赛，你也不舒服吗？

Hésài: Shì de. Wǒ hěn lèi, xiǎng shuì jiào.
何赛：是的。我很累，想睡觉。

我今天不舒服 8

Miss Wang: Hesai, are you also not feeling well?

Hesai: No. I'm very tired. I want to sleep.

(四) 08-4

Wǒ jīntiān bù shūfu, lā dùzi, bù xiǎng shàng kè, xiǎng xiūxi.
我今天不舒服，拉肚子，不想 上课，想休息。

I'm not feeling well today. I have diarrhea. I don't want to attend class. I want to rest.

生词 New words

1	了	le	part.	used at the end of a sentence to indicate the completion of an action or a change	
2	肚子	dùzi	n.	stomach, belly	
3	疼	téng	adj.	painful	肚子疼 / 妹妹肚子疼 / 妈妈肚子疼
4	舒服	shūfu	adj.	comfortable	肚子不舒服 / 很舒服 / 跑步很舒服
5	拉肚子	lā dùzi		to have diarrhea	
6	能	néng	v.	can	不能 / 能打篮球 / 不能打篮球
7	来	lái	v.	to come	来教室 / 来上课 / 来听音乐
8	累	lèi	adj.	tired	很累 / 不累
9	想	xiǎng	v.	to want	想玩儿 / 想睡觉 / 想吃饭
10	休息	xiūxi	v.	to rest	想休息

习写字 Learn to write the characters

shū
easy, leisurely

fú
to be accustomed to

dù
stomach, belly

zi
a suffix

téng

lā
to defecate

néng

lái

lèi

xiǎng

xiū
to rest

息
xī
to stop

交际功能 Communicative functions

1. **询问是否不舒服** To ask if someone is not feeling well

   "你怎么了?" 询问对方是否不舒服。

   "你怎么了?" is used to ask if someone is not feeling well.

2. **述说身体不舒服** To describe physical discomfort

   "我不舒服。"述说身体不舒服。也可以回答得具体些,"我拉肚子。""我很累。"等。

   "我不舒服。" is used to describe physical discomfort. The answer can be more specific, such as "我拉肚子。" and "我很累。".

3. 表达情况发生了变化 To indicate a change of the condition

句尾"了"表达情况发生了变化。如"她拉肚子了。"表示"她"的情况发生了变化,即以前没有拉肚子,现在拉肚子。

"了" is used at the end of a sentence to express a change of the condition. For example, "她拉肚子了。" indicates that her condition has changed and that she did not have diarrhea before but have it now.

(1)我累了,不想去上课。
(2)他睡觉了。

4. 表达不能做某事 To indicate inability to do something

"不能+动词",表示没有能力做某事。如"今天她不能来上课。"表达能做某事时用"能",如"今天她能来上课。""我能早上六点起床。"

"不能 + verb" is used to express the inability to do something, such as "今天她不能来上课。".
"能" is used to express the ability to do something, such as "今天她能来上课。" and "我能早上六点起床。".

5. 表达想做某事 To indicate inclination to do something

"想+动词或动词短语",表示想做某事。

"想 + verb / verb phrase" is used to express the inclination to do something.

(1)我很累,想休息。
(2)我想睡觉。
(3)我想听音乐。
(4)我想玩儿电脑游戏。

6. 表达不想做某事 To indicate disinclination to do something

"不想+动词或动词短语",表示不想做某事。如"不想上课、不想睡觉、不想玩儿游戏"。

"不想 + verb / verb phrase" is used to express the disinclination to do something. For example: "不想上课","不想睡觉","不想玩儿游戏".

7. 表达转述 To relate something as told by another

"她说她今天不能来上课。"表达转述。"她说"后面的话"她今天不能来上课"是转述的内容。

"她说今天她不能来上课。" is used to relate something as told by another. "她说" is followed by "今天她不能来上课", the words said by another.

（1）老师说明天没有课。

（2）田中说全真爱今天不舒服。

补充词语 Supplementary words

1	头	tóu	n.	head
2	嗓子	sǎngzi	n.	throat
3	生病	shēng bìng	v.	to get ill
4	发烧	fā shāo	v.	to have a fever
5	咳嗽	késou	v.	to cough
6	感冒	gǎnmào	v./n.	to have a cold; cold
7	医生	yīshēng	n.	doctor
8	请假	qǐng jià	v.	to ask for leave

第九课 我买苹果
Dì-jiǔ kè Wǒ mǎi píngguǒ
Lesson 9 I want to buy apples

交际功能 Communicative functions

1. 询问购物意愿 To ask about someone's shopping intention：您买什么？
2. 询问价钱 To ask about the price：苹果怎么卖？/ 苹果多少钱一斤？
3. 人民币的读法 The way to read RMB

课文 Text

(一) 09-1

全真爱(Quán Zhēn'ài)：你去哪儿？(Nǐ qù nǎr?)

何赛(Hésài)：我去买东西。(Wǒ qù mǎi dōngxi.)

Quan Zhen'ai: Where are you going?

Hesai: I'm going shopping.

(二) 09-2

售货员(shòuhuòyuán)（Salesman）：您买什么？(Nín mǎi shénme?)

田中(Tiánzhōng)：我买苹果。(Wǒ mǎi píngguǒ.)

Salesman: Can I help you?

Tianzhong: I want to buy apples.

(三) 09-3

何赛(Hésài)：请问，苹果怎么卖？(Qǐngwèn, píngguǒ zěnme mài?)

售货员(shòuhuòyuán)：四块钱一斤。您要多少？(Sì kuài qián yì jīn. Nín yào duōshao?)

何赛(Hésài)：我要两斤。一共多少钱？(Wǒ yào liǎng jīn. Yígòng duōshao qián?)

售货员(shòuhuòyuán)：一共八块钱。(Yígòng bā kuài qián.)

Hesai: Excuse me, how much are the apples?

Salesman: Four *yuan* half a kilo. How many would you like?

Hesai: I want a kilo. How much in total?

Salesman: 8 *yuan* in total.

(四) 09-4

Wǒ xǐhuan chī shuǐguǒ, jīntiān wǒ mǎile hěn duō shuǐguǒ, yígòng huāle
我喜欢吃水果，今天我买了很多水果，一共花了 22.50
yuán (èrshí'èr kuài wǔ máo).
元（二十二块五毛）。

I like to eat fruits. I bought a lot of fruits today and spent 22.50 *yuan* in total.

生词 New words

1	您	nín	pron.	(*formal, honorific*) you	您好 / 您家 / 我和您
2	买	mǎi	v.	to buy	买水果 / 买篮球 / 买电脑
3	苹果	píngguǒ	n.	apple	一个苹果 / 买苹果 / 吃苹果
4	卖	mài	v.	to sell	卖苹果 / 怎么卖 / 电脑怎么卖
5	块	kuài	m.	*kuai*, the colloquial form of *yuan*, the basic unit of money in China	一块 / 两块 / 四块四
6	钱	qián	n.	money	三块钱 / 十四块钱 / 四十四块钱
7	斤	jīn	m.	the basic unit of weight in China, equal to 500 grams	七斤 / 六斤 / 八十五斤
8	要	yào	v.	to want	你要什么 / 我要苹果
9	多少	duōshao	pron.	how many, how much	多少钱 / 要多少 / 买多少

10	一共	yígòng	adv.	altogether, in total	一共三块 / 一共九十块钱 / 一共十斤
11	水果	shuǐguǒ	n.	fruit	买水果 / 卖水果 / 吃水果 / 很多水果
12	了	le	part.	used after a verb or an adjective to indicate the completion of an actual or expected action or a change	买了很多水果 / 吃了午饭 / 卖了十斤苹果
13	多	duō	adj.	many, much, more	很多 / 很多苹果 / 很多中学生
14	花	huā	v.	to spend	花钱 / 花很多钱 / 花了十块钱
15	元	yuán	m.	*yuan*, the basic unit of money in China	一元 / 两元 / 五十元
16	毛	máo	m.	*mao*, a fractional unit of money in China, ten cents	一毛 / 五毛

习写字 Learn to write the characters

nín

mǎi

mài

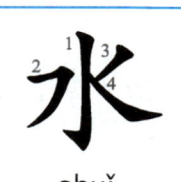
shuǐ
water

guǒ
fruit

qián

duō
many, much, more

shǎo
few, little, less

yào

gòng
total

le

huā

我买苹果 9

交际功能 Communicative functions

1. 询问购物意愿 To ask about someone's shopping intention

"您买什么？"询问购物意愿。

"您买什么？" is used to ask about someone's shopping intention.

2. 询问价钱 To ask about the price

"苹果怎么卖？"用于询问苹果的价钱，也可以说"苹果多少钱一斤？"

"苹果怎么卖？" is used to ask about the price of apples. You can also say "苹果多少钱一斤？".

3. 人民币的读法 The way to read RMB

人民币有三个单位：元、角（jiǎ）、分（fēn）。口语里也读作：块（kuài）、毛（máo）、分。下面是人民币的读法：

There are three units in RMB, i.e. *yuan*, *jiao* and *fen*, which are respectively *kuai*, *mao* and *fen* in spoken Chinese. RMB is read in the following ways:

4.00 元读作四块钱，或四块

8.50 元读作八块五毛钱，或八块五

"4.00 *yuan*" is read as "sì kuài qián", or "sì kuài".

"8.50 *yuan*" is read as "bā kuài wǔ máo qián", or "bā kuài wǔ".

补充词语 Supplementary words

1	香蕉	xiāngjiāo	n.	banana
2	梨	lí	n.	pear
3	橙子	chéngzi	n.	orange
4	葡萄	pútao	n.	grape
5	芒果	mángguǒ	n.	mango

第十课 这是包子
Lesson 10 These are steamed stuffed buns

交际功能 Communicative functions

1. 询问事物名称 To ask the name of something：这是什么？/那是什么？
2. 点菜 To order food：我要一个西红柿炒鸡蛋、一碗米饭、一瓶可乐。
3. 表达某种食物好吃 To indicate some food is delicious：中国菜很好吃。

这是包子 10

课文 Text

(一) 🔊 10-1

Hésài: Zhè shì shénme?
何赛：这是什么？

Dàwèi: Zhè shì bāozi.
大卫：这是包子。

Hésài: Nà shì shénme?
何赛：那是什么？

Dàwèi: Nà shì jiǎozi.
大卫：那是饺子。

Hesai: What are these?

Dawei: These are steamed stuffed buns.

Hesai: What are those?

Dawei: Those are dumplings.

(二) 🔊 10-2

fúwùyuán: Nín yào shénme?
服务员：您要什么？

Dàwèi: Wǒ yào yí fèn jiǎozi.
大卫：我要一份饺子。

fúwùyuán: Èrshíwǔ yuán. Nín yě yào jiǎozi ma?
服务员：二十五元。您也要饺子吗？

Hésài: Bù, wǒ yào yí gè xīhóngshì chǎo jīdàn, yì wǎn mǐfàn, yì píng kělè.
何赛：不，我要一个西红柿炒鸡蛋、一碗米饭、一瓶可乐。

fúwùyuán: Hǎo de, yígòng èrshíbā yuán.
服务员：好的，一共二十八元。

Waitress: May I take your order?

Dawei: I would like dumplings.

Waitress: 25 *yuan*. Would you also like dumplings?

Hesai: No. I would like tomatoes with scrambled eggs, a bowl of rice and a bottle of Coke.

Waitress: OK, 28 *yuan* in total.

(三) 🔊 10-3

fúwùyuán: Nín yào shénme?
服务员：您要什么？

Quán Zhēn'ài: Wǒ yào sì gè bāozi.
全真爱：我要四个包子。

Waitress: May I take your order?

Quan Zhen'ai: I would like four steamed stuffed buns.

(四) 🔊 10-4

Jīntiān wǎnshang wǒ chīle zhōngguócài, hěn hǎochī.
今天晚上我吃了中国菜，很好吃。

I had Chinese food for dinner. It was delicious!

生词 New words

1	这	zhè	pron.	this	
2	包子	bāozi	n.	steamed stuffed bun	一个包子
3	那	nà	pron.	that	

这是包子 10

4	饺子	jiǎozi	n.	dumpling	一个饺子 / 一斤饺子
5	份	fèn	m.	portion, serving	一份饺子
6	西红柿	xīhóngshì	n.	tomato	一个西红柿 / 几个西红柿 / 吃西红柿
7	炒	chǎo	v.	to fry	炒西红柿 / 炒鸡蛋
8	鸡蛋	jīdàn	n.	egg	吃鸡蛋 / 一个鸡蛋 / 西红柿炒鸡蛋
	鸡	jī	n.	chicken	
	蛋	dàn	n.	egg	
9	碗	wǎn	n.	bowl	
10	米饭	mǐfàn	n.	(cooked) rice	一碗米饭 / 一份米饭 / 鸡蛋炒米饭
	米	mǐ	n.	rice	
11	瓶	píng	n.	bottle	一瓶 / 几瓶
12	可乐	kělè	n.	Coke	一瓶可乐 / 几瓶可乐
13	中国菜	zhōngguócài		Chinese food	
	菜	cài	n.	food, dish	
14	好吃	hǎochī	adj.	delicious	很好吃 / 好吃的菜 / 好吃的中国菜

习写字 Learn to write the characters

bāo
package

fèn

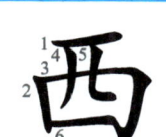
xī
west

hóng
red

jī

dàn

píng

kě
can, may

lè
happy, glad

wǎn

mǐ

cài

交际功能 Communicative functions

1. 询问事物名称 To ask the name of something

"这是什么?""那是什么?"询问事物名称。

"这是什么?" and "那是什么?" are used to ask the name of something.

2. 点菜 To order food

"我要……。"点菜。

"我要……。" is used to order food.

（1）我要一个西红柿炒鸡蛋。

（2）我要一碗米饭。

（3）我要一瓶可乐。

3. 表达某种食物好吃 To indicate some food is delicious

"……很好吃。"表达某种食物好吃。

"……很好吃。" is used to express that something is delicious.

补充词语 Supplementary words

1	面条儿	miàntiáor	n.	noodle(s)
2	盘	pán	m.	plate
3	饮料	yǐnliào	n.	beverage
4	冰水	bīng shuǐ		ice water
5	喝	hē	v.	to drink
6	筷子	kuàizi	n.	chopstick(s)

第十一课 你可以坐地铁去故宫
Lesson 11 You can take the subway to the Imperial Palace

交际功能 Communicative functions

1. 问路 To ask the way：去地铁站怎么走？
2. 指路 To show the way：往前走。
3. 询问如何去某地 To ask the way to somewhere：请问，我怎么去故宫？
4. 表达去某地的方式 To indicate how to go somewhere：坐地铁去故宫
5. 表示动作发生得快、顺利，用时短 To indicate an action is quick and smooth：往前走五分钟就到了。
6. 表示条件许可做某事 To indicate someone can do something as the condition permits：你可以坐地铁去故宫。
7. 称说时段 The expression of duration

课文 Text

(一) 🔊 11-1

Quán Zhēn'ài: Qǐngwèn, qù dìtiězhàn zěnme zǒu?
全真爱：请问，去地铁站怎么走？

lùrén: Wǎng qián zǒu wǔ fēnzhōng jiù dào le.
路　人：往前走五分钟就到了。

Quán Zhēn'ài: Xièxie.
全真爱：谢谢。

lùrén: Búyòng xiè.
路　人：不用谢。

Quan Zhen'ai: Excuse me, how can I get to the subway station?

Passer-by: Walk ahead for five minutes and you will get there.

Quan Zhen'ai: Thank you.

Passer-by: You're welcome.

(二) 🔊 11-2

Tiánzhōng: Qǐngwèn, wǒ zěnme qù Gùgōng?
田　中：请问，我怎么去故宫？

Wáng lǎoshī: Nǐ kěyǐ zuò dìtiě qù, bàn xiǎoshí jiù dào le.
王老师：你可以坐地铁去，半小时就到了。

Tiánzhōng: Xièxie.
田　中：谢谢。

Wáng lǎoshī: Bú kèqi.
王老师：不客气。

Tianzhong: Excuse me, how can I get to the Imperial Palace?

11 你可以坐地铁去故宫

Miss Wang: You can take the subway. It takes only half an hour to get there.

Tianzhong: Thank you.

Miss Wang: You're welcome.

(三) 11-3

何赛：老师，我可以坐公交车去故宫吗？
Hésài: Lǎoshī, wǒ kěyǐ zuò gōngjiāochē qù Gùgōng ma?

王老师：可以。
Wáng lǎoshī: Kěyǐ.

Hesai: Miss Wang, can I take a bus to the Imperial Palace?

Miss Wang: Yes, you can.

(四) 11-4

我想去故宫，老师说我可以坐地铁去，也可以打车去。
Wǒ xiǎng qù Gùgōng, lǎoshī shuō wǒ kěyǐ zuò dìtiě qù, yě kěyǐ dǎ chē qù.

I want to go to the Imperial Palace. The teacher said that I could take the subway or a taxi to go there.

生词 New words

1	去	qù	v.	to go	去卫生间 / 去教室
2	地铁站	dìtiězhàn	n.	subway station	
	地铁	dìtiě	n.	subway	坐地铁
	站	zhàn	n.	station	
3	走	zǒu	v.	to walk	怎么走
4	往	wǎng	prep.	to, towards	
5	前	qián	n.	front, ahead	往前 / 往前走

6	分钟	fēnzhōng	n.	minute	十分钟
7	就	jiù	adv.	just, only	十分钟就到
8	到	dào	v.	to arrive, to reach	到教室去 / 到了
9	不用	búyòng	adv.	need not	
10	故宫	Gùgōng	p.n.	the Imperial Palace	去故宫
11	可以	kěyǐ	v.	can, may	可以坐地铁 / 可以打车 / 可以去
12	小时	xiǎoshí	n.	hour	半个小时 / 一个小时 / 一个半小时
13	公交车	gōngjiāochē	n.	bus	坐公交车 / 公交车站
	公交	gōngjiāo	n.	public traffic	
	车	chē	n.	vehicle	
14	打车	dǎ chē	v.	to take a taxi	打车去故宫

习写字 Learn to write the characters

去 qù

地 dì — ground

铁 tiě — iron; railway

往 wǎng

前 qián

走 zǒu

到 dào

以 yǐ — with, by

坐 zuò — to sit

半 bàn — half

小 xiǎo — small

时 shí — time

打 dǎ — to take (a taxi)

车 chē

11 你可以坐地铁去故宫

交际功能 Communicative functions

1. 问路 To ask the way

"去地铁站怎么走？"询问怎么去地铁站。

"去地铁站怎么走？" is used to ask the way to the subway station.

2. 指路 To show the way

"往＋方位词＋走"指路。

"往＋ noun of direction or locality ＋走" is used to show the way.

3. 询问如何去某地 To ask the way to somewhere

"请问，我怎么去故宫？"询问如何去故宫。

"请问，我怎么去故宫？" is used to ask the way to the Imperial Palace.

4. 表达去某地的方式 To indicate how to go somewhere

"方式＋'去'＋某地"，表达去某地的方式。如"坐地铁去故宫"，"坐地铁"是"去故宫"的方式。

"The way ＋'去'＋ somewhere" is used to indicate how to go somewhere. For example, in "坐地铁去故宫"，"坐地铁" is the way of "去故宫".

（1）我们坐公交车去故宫。

（2）我们打车去故宫。

5. 表示动作发生得快、顺利，用时短 To indicate an action is quick and smooth

"就"用在动词前，表示这个动作发生得快、顺利，用的时间短，一般有时段词。如，"往前走五分钟就到了。"

When used before a verb, "就" indicates that an action takes place quickly and smoothly. A word of duration is usually used. For example: "往前走五分钟就到了。".

（1）我走了三分钟就到教室了。

（2）坐地铁去故宫，半个小时就到了。

6. 表示条件许可做某事 To indicate someone can do something as the condition permits

"'可以'+动词",表示条件许可。

"'可以'+ verb" indicates that the condition permits.

(1) 你可以坐公交车去故宫。

(2) 今天你不舒服,可以不去上课。

7. 称说时段 The expression of duration

用"数词+'小时/分钟/天/年'"称说时段。如"半小时/半个小时、五分钟、两天、三年"。

" Numeral +'小时/分钟/天/年'" is used to indicate a period of time. For example: "半小时/半个小时","五分钟","两天", and "三年".

补充词语 Supplementary words

1	左	n.	zuǒ	left
2	右	n.	yòu	right
3	后	n.	hòu	back
4	图书馆	n.	túshūguǎn	library
5	机场	n.	jīchǎng	airport
6	饭馆	n.	fànguǎn	restaurant
7	走路	v.	zǒu lù	to walk

第十二课 今天天气不错
Lesson 12　The weather is good today

交际功能 Communicative functions

1. 谈论天气 To talk about the weather：今天天气不错，不冷也不热。/ 昨天太热了。
2. 询问天气情况 To ask about the weather：明天天气怎么样？
3. 表达转述 To relate something as told by another：听说明天会下雨。
4. 表达程度很高 To indicate a high degree：昨天太热了。
5. "会"表示可能 "会" indicating a possibility：明天会下雨。

课文 Text

(一) 12-1

Dàwèi: Jīntiān tiānqì búcuò, bù lěng yě bú rè.
大卫：今天天气不错，不冷也不热。

Tiánzhōng: Shì de. Hěn shūfu.
田中：是的。很舒服。

Dàwèi: Zuótiān tài rè le.
大卫：昨天太热了。

Dawei: The weather is good today. It's neither too cold nor too hot.

Tianzhong: I agree. It's very comfortable.

Dawei: It was too hot yesterday.

(二) 12-2

Tiánzhōng: Míngtiān tiānqì zěnmeyàng?
田中：明天天气怎么样？

Dàwèi: Tīngshuō míngtiān huì xià yǔ.
大卫：听说明天会下雨。

Tianzhong: How's the weather tomorrow?

Dawei: I heard that it might rain tomorrow.

今天天气不错 12

(三) 🔊 12-3

Zuótiān hěn rè, jīntiān bù lěng yě bú rè, hěn shūfu. Tīngshuō míngtiān huì
昨天很热，今天不冷也不热，很舒服。听说 明天会
xià yǔ, wǒ bù xǐhuan xià yǔ.
下雨，我不喜欢下雨。

It was hot yesterday. It is neither too cold nor too hot today, and it's very comfortable. I heard that it might rain tomorrow. I don't like the rain.

生词 New words

1	天气	tiānqì	n.	weather	天气很好 / 天气不好
2	不错	búcuò	adj.	good, not bad	天气不错 / 菜不错 / 他的汉语不错
	错	cuò	adj.	wrong, bad	
3	冷	lěng	adj.	cold	不冷 / 很冷
4	热	rè	adj.	hot	不冷也不热 / 很热
5	昨天	zuótiān	n.	yesterday	昨天星期一 / 昨天天气很好 / 昨天我吃了中国菜
6	太……了	tài…le		too, extremely	太热了 / 太好了 / 太累了
7	怎么样	zěnmeyàng	pron.	how about	天气怎么样 / 中国菜怎么样 / 故宫怎么样
8	听说	tīngshuō	v.	to hear of	听说你不舒服 / 听说故宫不错
9	会	huì	v.	can, might	
10	下雨	xià yǔ		to rain	下雨了 / 明天会下雨 / 今天不会下雨
	雨	yǔ	n.	rain	今天有雨

65

习写字 Learn to write the characters

cuò

lěng

rè

de
a particle

zuó
yesterday

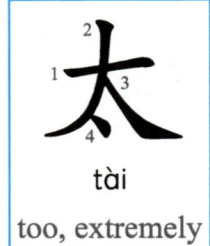
tài
too, extremely

zěn
why, how

me
a suffix

yàng
appearance

huì

yǔ

交际功能 Communicative functions

1. 谈论天气 To talk about the weather

"今天天气不错。"表达天气好。

"今天天气不错。" is used to indicate the weather is good.

2. 询问天气情况 To ask about the weather

"怎么样"询问情况。如,"明天天气怎么样?"询问明天天气情况。又如,"你买的苹果怎么样?"询问苹果的情况。

"怎么样" is used to ask about the condition. For example, "明天天气怎么样?" is used to ask about the weather tomorrow, and "你买的苹果怎么样?" is used to ask how the apples are.

3. 表达转述 To relate something as told by another

"听说……"表达转述。如,"听说明天会下雨。"中"明天会下雨"是转述的内容。一般不用说明来源。

"听说……" is used to relate something as told by another. For example, in "听说明天会下雨。", "明天会下雨" is what is related. It is not necessary to point out the source.

（1）听说明天很热。

（2）听说他妈妈会说汉语。

4. 表达程度很高 To indicate a high degree

"太……了"表达程度很高,"太"后面一般是形容词。如,"昨天太热了。"

"'太'＋形容词＋'了'",一般含有不如意、不满意的意思。

"太……了" is used to indicate a high degree of something, and "太" is usually followed by an adjective. For example: "昨天太热了。".

"太 + adj. + 了" usually implies dissatisfaction.

（1）第十课的生词太多了。

（2）今天我太累了。

5. "会"表示可能 "会" indicating a possibility

"'会'＋动词",表示有可能发生的动作。如,"明天会下雨。"意思是明天有可能下雨。

"会 + verb" indicates a possible action. For example, "明天会下雨。" means that it might rain tomorrow.

补充词语 Supplementary words

#	词	拼音	词性	英文
1	下雪	xià xuě		to snow
	雪	xuě	n.	snow
2	刮风	guā fēng		to be windy
	风	fēng	n.	wind
3	大雨	dàyǔ	n.	heavy rain
	大	dà	adj.	big, heavy (rain, etc.)
4	小雨	xiǎoyǔ	n.	light rain
	小	xiǎo	adj.	small
5	太阳	tàiyang	n.	sun
6	多云	duōyún	n.	cloudy
	云	yún	n.	cloud
7	晴	qíng	adj.	sunny
8	阴	yīn	adj.	overcast
9	凉快	liángkuai	adj.	cool
10	暖和	nuǎnhuo	adj.	warm
11	度	dù	num.	degree (of intensity, hardness, heat, etc.)
12	春天	chūntiān	n.	spring
13	夏天	xiàtiān	n.	summer
14	秋天	qiūtiān	n.	autumn
15	冬天	dōngtiān	n.	winter

第十三课　我喜欢白色　Lesson 13　I like white

Dì-shísān kè　　Wǒ xǐhuan báisè

交际功能 Communicative functions

1. 询问喜欢的颜色 To ask about the color someone likes：你喜欢什么颜色？
2. 表达喜欢的颜色 To indicate the color someone likes：我喜欢红色。
3. 选择提问 Alternative questions：你喜欢红色还是喜欢绿色？
4. 称说颜色 The expression of colors

课文 Text

（一） 🔊 13-1

Quán Zhēn'ài: Nǐ xǐhuan shénme yánsè?
全真爱：你喜欢什么颜色？

Tiánzhōng: Wǒ xǐhuan báisè.
田 中：我喜欢白色。

Quan Zhen'ai: What color do you like?

Tianzhong: I like white.

（二） 🔊 13-2

Dàwèi: Nǐ xǐhuan hóngsè háishi xǐhuan lǜsè?
大卫：你喜欢红色还是喜欢绿色？

Hésài: Wǒ xǐhuan lǜsè.
何赛：我喜欢绿色。

Dawei: Do you prefer red or green?

Hesai: I prefer green.

（三） 🔊 13-3

Quán Zhēn'ài: Nǐ de bái chènshān zhēn piàoliang.
全真爱：你的白衬衫真漂亮。

Tiánzhōng: Xièxie. Nǐ de lán niúzǎikù yě hěn piàoliang.
田 中：谢谢。你的蓝牛仔裤也很漂亮。

Quán Zhēn'ài: Wǒ xǐhuan lánsè.
全真爱：我喜欢蓝色。

Quan Zhen'ai: Your white shirt looks very nice.

Tianzhong: Thank you. Your blue jeans also look nice.

Quan Zhen'ai: I like blue.

(四) 13-4

Wǒ xǐhuan hóngsè hé hēisè, wǒ xǐhuan chuān hóng T xù hé hēi niúzǎikù.
我喜欢红色和黑色，我喜欢穿 红T恤和黑牛仔裤。

I like red and black. I like to wear a red T-shirt and black jeans.

生词 New words

1	颜色	yánsè	n.	color	什么颜色 / 水果的颜色
	色	sè		color	
2	白色	báisè	n.	white	白色的衬衫
	白	bái	adj.	white	
3	红色	hóngsè	n.	red	喜欢红色 / 红色的苹果 / 红色的西红柿
	红	hóng	adj.	red	
4	还是	háishi	conj.	or	红色还是白色 / 坐地铁还是打车 / 下雨还是下雪
5	绿色	lǜsè	n.	green	喜欢绿色 / 绿色的水果
	绿	lǜ	adj.	green	
6	衬衫	chènshān	n.	shirt	白衬衫 / 红衬衫
7	真	zhēn	adv.	really	真不错 / 真热
8	漂亮	piàoliang	adj.	beautiful, pretty	真漂亮 / 太漂亮了 / 漂亮的衬衫
9	蓝	lán	adj.	blue	蓝色 / 蓝衬衫 / 蓝天

10	牛仔裤	niúzǎikù	n.	jeans	喜欢牛仔裤 / 白色的牛仔裤
	牛仔	niúzǎi	n.	cowboy	
	裤	kù		trousers, pants	
11	黑色	hēisè	n.	black	黑色的牛仔裤
	黑	hēi	adj.	black	黑衬衫
12	穿	chuān	v.	to wear	穿白衬衫 / 穿牛仔裤
13	T恤	T xù		T-shirt	白T恤 / 穿T恤 / 买T恤

习写字 Learn to write the characters

hóng

lǜ

bái

hēi

lán

yán
color

sè

zhēn

piào
a bound morpheme

liàng
bright, light

hái
still

chèn
to put a lining inside sth.

shān
unlined upper garment

kù

交际功能 Communicative functions

1. 询问喜欢的颜色 To ask about the color someone likes

"你喜欢什么颜色？"询问喜欢的颜色。

"你喜欢什么颜色？" is used to ask about the color someone likes.

2. 表达喜欢的颜色 To indicate the color someone likes

"我喜欢红色。"表达喜欢的颜色。

"我喜欢红色。" is used to indicate the color someone likes.

3. 选择提问 Alternative questions

"还是"选择提问。如"你喜欢红色还是喜欢绿色？"，希望对方在"喜欢红色""喜欢绿色"两者中选择一项回答。

"还是" is used in alternative questions. For example, when asking "你喜欢红色还是喜欢绿色？", the replier is expected to choose between "喜欢红色" and "喜欢绿色".

（1）你是韩国人还是日本人？

（2）你喜欢吃中国菜还是喜欢吃日本菜？

4. 称说颜色 The expression of colors

用"～色"称说颜色，如"白色、蓝色、黑色、红色"等。"色"也可以省略，如"白衬衫、蓝牛仔裤"。

"～色" can be used as the expression of colors. For example: "白色","蓝色","黑色","红色", etc. "色" can also be omitted. For example: "白衬衫","蓝牛仔裤".

补充词语 Supplementary words

1	黄	huáng	adj.	yellow
2	灰	huī	adj.	gray
3	衣服	yīfu	n.	clothes
4	裤子	kùzi	n.	trousers, pants
5	短裤	duǎnkù	n.	shorts
6	袜子	wàzi	n.	socks
7	帽子	màozi	n.	hat
8	件	jiàn	m.	piece (*used for clothes*)
9	双	shuāng	m.	pair (*used for shoes, socks, etc.*)
10	条	tiáo	m.	pair, piece (*used for pants, skirts, etc.*)

第十四课 我会说一点儿汉语
Dì-shísì kè   Wǒ huì shuō yìdiǎnr Hànyǔ
Lesson 14 I can speak a little Chinese

交际功能 Communicative functions

1. 询问会说何种语言 To ask about someone's ability to speak a language：你会说汉语吗？
2. 表达外语水平 To indicate someone's foreign language proficiency：我会说一点儿汉语。
3. 询问学习时间 To ask about someone's duration of study：你学了多长时间汉语了？
4. 说明动作持续的时间 To indicate the duration of an action：我学了半年汉语了。
5. 表达学习体会 To indicate someone's learning experience：我觉得汉语声调很难。
6. 表达称赞 To praise someone：你的汉语真不错。
7. 表达谦虚 To show modesty：哪里哪里，马马虎虎。
8. 加强语气 To emphasize the tone：学习汉语挺有意思的。

课文 Text

(一) 🔊 14-1

lùrén: Nǐ huì shuō Hànyǔ ma?
路人：你会说汉语吗？

Hésài: Huì shuō yìdiǎnr.
何赛：会说一点儿。

Passer-by: Can you speak Chinese?

Hesai: Yes, I can speak a little.

(二) 🔊 14-2

Tiánzhōng: Nǐ xuéle duō cháng shíjiān Hànyǔ le?
田中：你学了多长时间汉语了？

Dàwèi: Wǒ xuéle bàn nián Hànyǔ le.
大卫：我学了半年汉语了。

Tiánzhōng: Nǐ de Hànyǔ zhēn búcuò.
田中：你的汉语真不错。

Dàwèi: Nǎli nǎli, mǎmǎhūhū.
大卫：哪里哪里，马马虎虎。

Tianzhong: How long have you been studying Chinese?

Dawei: I have been studying it for half a year.

Tianzhong: Your Chinese is pretty good.

Dawei: It's OK.

(三) 🔊 14-3

Wáng lǎoshī: Nǐmen juéde Hànyǔ nán xué ma?
王 老师：你们觉得汉语难学吗？

Hésài: Wǒ juéde Hànyǔ shēngdiào hěn nán.
何 赛：我觉得汉语声调很难。

Dàwèi: Wǒ juéde Hànzì hěn nán.
大 卫：我觉得汉字很难。

Miss Wang: Do you think Chinese is difficult?

Hesai: I think that Chinese tones are difficult.

Dawei: I think that Chinese characters are difficult.

(四) 🔊 14-4

Wǒ xuéle sān gè xīngqī Hànyǔ le. Wǒ juéde Hànyǔ hěn hǎotīng, Hànzì hěn
我学了三个星期汉语了。我觉得汉语很好听，汉字很

hǎokàn. Wǒ xǐhuan shuō Hànyǔ, xiě Hànzì, yě xǐhuan chàng zhōngwéngē. Xuéxí
好看。我喜欢说汉语、写汉字，也喜欢唱中文歌。学习

Hànyǔ tǐng yǒu yìsi de.
汉语挺有意思的。

I have been studying Chinese for three weeks. I think that Chinese sounds great and Chinese characters are very beautiful. I enjoy speaking and writing Chinese, and singing Chinese songs. It's very interesting to study Chinese.

生词 New words

1	会	huì	v.	can, to be able to	会说汉语 / 会打篮球 / 不会 / 不会唱歌
2	一点儿	yìdiǎnr	num.-cl.	a little	说一点儿汉语 / 吃一点儿 / 买了一点儿东西
3	学	xué	v.	to study, to learn	学汉语 / 学唱歌 / 学好
4	多长	duō cháng		how long	
	多	duō	pron.	what, how	多大
	长	cháng	adj.	long	长时间 / 长裤 / 很长 / 不长
5	时间	shíjiān	n.	time	有时间 / 没时间 / 多长时间
6	哪里	nǎli	pron.	a modest expression usually used after being praised	哪里哪里
7	马马虎虎	mǎmǎhūhū	adj.	a modest expression usually used after being praised	我的汉语马马虎虎 / 他的英语马马虎虎
8	觉得	juéde	v.	to feel	觉得热 / 觉得很累 / 觉得不舒服 / 觉得很快
9	难	nán	adj.	difficult	很难 / 太难了 / 不难 / 不太难
10	声调	shēngdiào	n.	tone	四个声调
	声	shēng	n.	voice, sound	
	调	diào	n.	tone	
11	汉字	Hànzì	p.n.	Chinese character	一个汉字 / 写汉字
12	好听	hǎotīng	adj.	pleasant to hear	很好听 / 不好听 / 觉得好听 / 他唱歌很好听
13	好看	hǎokàn	adj.	beautiful, good-looking	衣服好看 / 照片好看 / 颜色很好看 / 不好看
	看	kàn	v.	to look	
14	写	xiě	v.	to write	写汉字 / 写字

15	中文歌	zhōngwéngē		Chinese song	
	中文	Zhōngwén	p.n.	Chinese language	中文书 / 中文电影 / 学中文 / 中文不难
	歌	gē	n.	song	唱歌 / 中文歌 / 英文歌
16	挺	tǐng	adv.	quite	挺好 / 挺难 / 挺有意思
17	意思	yìsi	n.	meaning, interest	这个汉字的意思 / 有意思 / 没意思

习写字 Learn to write the characters

cháng

nián
year

jué
to feel

de
a particle

nán

shēng

diào

lǐ
in, inside

mǎ
horse

hǔ
tiger

xiě

chàng
to sing

gē

交际功能 Communicative functions

1. 询问会说何种语言 To ask about someone's ability to speak a language

"你会说～语吗？"询问会不会说某种语言。

"你会说～语吗？" is used to ask if one can speak a certain language.

（1）你会说汉语吗？
（2）你会说英语吗？
（3）你会说日语吗？

2. 表达外语水平 To indicate someone's foreign language proficiency

"我会说一点儿汉语。"说明自己的汉语水平。

"我会说一点儿汉语。" is used to indicate someone's Chinese proficiency.

3. 询问学习时间 To ask about someone's duration of study

"你学了多长时间汉语了？"询问学习汉语的时间。"多长时间"可以用来询问动作持续的时间。

"你学了多长时间汉语了？" is used to ask about the duration of one's Chinese study. "多长时间" can be used to ask about the duration of an action.

（1）他打了多长时间篮球了？
（2）我们坐了多长时间地铁了？

4. 说明动作持续的时间 To indicate the duration of an action

表示时段的词语放在动词后面，说明动作持续的时间。句尾"了"表示这个动作还要继续。如"我学了半年汉语了。"，"半年"说明动词"学"持续了半年，句尾"了"说明"学"还在继续。

A verb can be followed by a word of duration to indicate the duration of an action. "了" at the end of a sentence indicates that the action may keep going. For example, in "我学了半年汉语了。"，"半年" indicates that the action of "学" has been lasting for half a year and "了" at the end of the sentence indicates that "学" is still ongoing.

（1）我坐了半个小时地铁了。
（2）他们打了两个小时篮球了。

5. 表达学习体会 To indicate someone's learning experience

"我觉得汉语声调很难。"表达学习汉语的体会。

"我觉得汉语声调很难。" is used to indicate someone's Chinese learning experience.

6. 表达称赞 To praise someone

"真不错"表达称赞。

" 真不错 " is used to praise others.

（1）你的汉语真不错。

还可以说：You can also say:

（2）他的汉语很好。

（3）你写的汉字真漂亮。

7. 表达谦虚 To show modesty

"哪里哪里，马马虎虎。"对别人的称赞表示谦虚。

" 哪里哪里，马马虎虎。" is used to show one's modesty when receiving praise from someone else.

8. 加强语气 To emphasize the tone

"学习汉语挺有意思的。"句尾"的"加强语气。

" 的 " at the end of " 学习汉语挺有意思的。" is used to emphasize the tone.

补充词语 Supplementary words

| 1 | 虽然 | suīrán | conj. | although |
| 2 | 但是 | dànshì | conj. | but |

Dì-shíwǔ kè　Yílù píng'ān
第十五课　一路平安　Lesson 15　Have a safe journey

交际功能 Communicative functions

1. 表达即将发生的动作 To indicate an upcoming action：我今天晚上就要回国了。
2. 询问动作发生的时间 To ask when an action will be taken：你什么时候回国？
3. 提出建议并希望同意 To make a proposal and hope the other party to agree：请告诉我你的邮箱，好吗？
4. 询问手机号码 To ask for someone's mobile phone number：你的手机号码是多少？
5. 表达选择 To indicate the options：我会给你发微信，或者发短信的。
6. 表达送行祝愿 To express one's wishes when seeing someone else off：一路平安。

一路平安 15

课文 Text

（一） 🔊 15-1

Dàwèi: Nǐ hǎo! Wǒ jīntiān wǎnshang jiù yào huí guó le. Nǐ shénme shíhou huí guó?
大卫：你好！我今天晚上就要回国了。你什么时候回国？

Tiánzhōng: Wǒ míngtiān huí guó.
田中：我明天回国。

Dawei: Hi! I'm going back to my motherland tonight. When will you go back to your motherland?

Tianzhong: I will go back tomorrow.

（二） 🔊 15-2

Dàwèi: Qǐng gàosu wǒ nǐ de yóuxiāng, hǎo ma? Wǒ huí guó hòu gěi nǐ fā yóujiàn.
大卫：请告诉我你的邮箱，好吗？我回国后给你发邮件。

Tiánzhōng: Hǎo de. Wǒ de yóuxiāng shì tianzhong@100.com, nǐ de ne?
田中：好的。我的邮箱是 tianzhong@100.com，你的呢？

Dàwèi: Wǒ de yóuxiāng shì dawei@99.com.
大卫：我的邮箱是 dawei@99.com。

Dawei: Can I have your email address? I'll send you an email after I return to my motherland.

Tianzhong: Sure. My email address is tianzhong@100.com. What is yours?

Dawei: My email address is dawei@99.com.

（三） 🔊 15-3

Quán Zhēn'ài: Nǐ de shǒujī hàomǎ shì duōshao?
全真爱：你的手机号码是多少？

Tiánzhōng:　　　198765432001.
田　中：198765432001。

Quán Zhēn'ài:　Wǒ huì gěi nǐ fā wēixìn, huòzhě fā duǎnxìn de.
全真爱：我会给你发微信，或者发短信的。

Tiánzhōng:　　Hǎo de.
田　中：好的。

Quan Zhen'ai: What is your mobile phone number?

Tianzhong: 198765432001.

Quan Zhen'ai: I'll send you either a WeChat message or a text message.

Tianzhong: OK.

（四）  15-4

Dàwèi:　　　Yílù píng'ān.
大　卫：一路平安。

Quán Zhēn'ài:　Yílù píng'ān.
全真爱：一路平安。

Dawei: Have a safe journey.

Quan Zhen'ai: You too.

生词 New words

1	要	yào	v.	will	要走 / 要学汉语
2	回	huí	v.	to go back	回家 / 回学校 / 回教室 / 回国
3	时候	shíhou	n.	(duration of) time	什么时候 / 什么时候上课 / 什么时候回家 / 什么时候吃饭

一路平安 15

4	告诉	gàosu	v.	to tell	告诉我 / 告诉你 / 告诉朋友 / 告诉老师
5	邮箱	yóuxiāng	n.	email address	你的邮箱 / 我的邮箱 / 老师的邮箱
	邮	yóu	v.	to mail	
	箱	xiāng	n.	box	
6	给	gěi	prep.	for, to	
7	发	fā	v.	to send	发邮件
8	邮件	yóujiàn	n.	mail	写邮件 / 发邮件
9	手机	shǒujī	n.	mobile phone	我的手机 / 你的手机 / 好看的手机 / 谁的手机
	手	shǒu	n.	hand	
	机	jī		machine	
10	号码	hàomǎ	n.	number	手机号码
11	微信	wēixìn	n.	WeChat	发微信 / 加微信
12	或者	huòzhě	conj.	or	
13	短信	duǎnxìn	n.	message, text message	一个短信 / 发短信 / 给我发短信
	短	duǎn	adj.	short	
	信	xìn	n.	letter, message	
14	一路平安	yílù píng'ān		to have a safe journey	
	一路	yílù	n.	journey	
	平安	píng'ān	adj.	safe	

习写字 Learn to write the characters

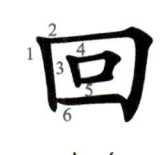
huí

gào
to tell

sù
to tell

yóu

xiāng

手
shǒu

 jī
 mǎ code
 duǎn
 xìn
 wēi tiny, little
 lù road

 píng peaceful, quiet
 ān safe

交际功能 Communicative functions

1. 表达即将发生的动作 To indicate an upcoming action

"要……了"表达即将发生的动作,说明动作在很短时间内即将发生,"要"前面常常加"就"。

"要……了" is used to indicate an upcoming action. "就" is often used before "要" to indicate that the action will happen in a short time.

(1) 我星期天就要回国了。

(2) 我们就要上课了。

(3) 天就要下雨了。

2. 询问动作发生的时间 To ask when an action will be taken

"'什么时候'+动词",询问动作发生的时间。

"'什么时候'+ verb" is used to ask when an action will be taken.

(1) 你什么时候回国?

(2) 你什么时候起床?

(3) 你什么时候吃晚饭?

3. 提出建议并希望同意 To make a proposal and hope the other party to agree

"……，好吗？"提出建议并希望对方同意。如"请告诉我你的邮箱，好吗？"，提出建议"告诉我你的邮箱"并希望对方同意。

"……，好吗？" is used to make a proposal and hope the other party to agree. For example, in "请告诉我你的邮箱，好吗？", the proposal "告诉我你的邮箱" is made and the other party's agreement is expected.

（1）中午吃包子，好吗？

（2）我们坐公交车去故宫，好吗？

4. 询问手机号码 To ask for someone's mobile phone number

"你的手机号码是多少？"询问手机号码。

"你的手机号码是多少？" is used to ask for someone's mobile phone number.

5. 表达选择 To indicate the options

"我会给你发微信，或者发短信的。""或者"连接"发微信""发短信"两个动词短语，表示选择。

In "我会给你发微信，或者发短信的。", "或者" connects the verb phrases "发微信" and "发短信" to indicate the options.

（1）星期六我喜欢和朋友去看电影，或者去买衣服。

（2）晚饭以后，我写作业，或者看电视。

6. 表达送行祝愿 To express one's wishes when seeing someone else off

"一路平安"送行祝愿用语。

"一路平安" is used to express one's wishes when seeing someone else off.

补充词语 Supplementary words

1	打电话	dǎ diànhuà		to phone sb.
	电话	diànhuà	n.	telephone
2	朋友圈	péngyouquān		WeChat Moments, an app function
3	写信	xiě xìn		to write a letter
4	欢迎	huānyíng	v.	to welcome
5	希望	xīwàng	v.	to hope, to wish

附录
Appendices

交际功能总表 Table of communicative functions

序号 / No.	英文 / English	汉语 / Chinese	课次 / Lesson
1	"会" indicating a possibility	"会"表示可能	12
2	Alternative questions	选择提问	13
3	The expression of colors	称说颜色	13
4	The expression of duration	称说时段	11
5	The expression of hobbies	称说爱好	7
6	The expression of major periods of time in a day	称说一天主要时间段	5
7	The expression of month/date/week	称说月、日、星期	6
8	The expression of numbers 1-10	称说数字 1—10	3
9	To address family members	称呼家庭成员	3
10	To ask about a location	询问处所	4
11	To ask about someone's ability to speak a language	询问会说何种语言	14
12	To ask about someone's birthday	询问生日	6
13	To ask about someone's duration of study	询问学习时间	14
14	To ask about someone's hobby	询问爱好	7
15	To ask about someone's identity	询问身份	2
16	To ask about someone's nationality	询问国籍	2
17	To ask about someone's shopping intention	询问购物意愿	9
18	To ask about the color someone likes	询问喜欢的颜色	13

序号 / No.	英文 / English	汉语 / Chinese	课次 / Lesson
19	To ask about the date	询问日期	6
20	To ask about the day of a week	询问星期几	6
21	To ask about the identity of a third person	询问第三者身份	2
22	To ask about the meaning of a word	询问词语的意思	4
23	To ask about the number of family members	询问家庭人口	3
24	To ask about the price	询问价钱	9
25	To ask about the time	询问时间	5
26	To ask about the weather	询问天气情况	12
27	To ask for someone's mobile phone number	询问手机号码	15
28	To ask how to say something in Chinese	询问用汉语怎么称说某物	4
29	To ask if someone is not feeling well	询问是否不舒服	8
30	To ask someone's name	询问姓名	1
31	To ask the name of something	询问事物名称	10
32	To ask the way	问路	11
33	To ask the way to somewhere	询问如何去某地	11
34	To ask when an action will be done	询问什么时间做什么事	5
35	To ask when an action will be taken	询问动作发生的时间	15
36	To confirm the information	确认信息	2
37	To correct the information	纠正信息	2
38	To describe physical discomfort	述说身体不舒服	8
39	To emphasize the tone	加强语气	14
40	To express gratitude	表达感谢	4
41	To express one's wishes when seeing someone else off	表达送行祝愿	15

序号 / No.	英文 / English	汉语 / Chinese	课次 / Lesson
42	To greet someone	见面打招呼	1
43	To indicate a change of the condition	表达情况发生了变化	8
44	To indicate a high degree	表达程度很高	12
45	To indicate an action is quick and smooth	表示动作发生得快、顺利，用时短	11
46	To indicate an upcoming action	表达即将发生的动作	15
47	To indicate disinclination to do something	表达不想做某事	8
48	To indicate having a certain family member	表达有某类家庭成员	3
49	To indicate how to go somewhere	表达去某地的方式	11
50	To indicate inability to do something	表达不能做某事	8
51	To indicate inclination to do something	表达想做某事	8
52	To indicate not having a certain family member	表达没有某类家庭成员	3
53	To indicate similarity	表达相同	2
54	To indicate someone's birthday	表达生日	6
55	To indicate some food is delicious	表达某种食物好吃	10
56	To indicate someone can do something as the condition permits	表示条件许可做某事	11
57	To indicate someone's foreign language proficiency	表达外语水平	14
58	To indicate someone's hobby	表达爱好	7
59	To indicate someone's learning experience	表达学习体会	14
60	To indicate the color someone likes	表达喜欢的颜色	13
61	To indicate the date	表达日期	6
62	To indicate the day of a week	表达星期几	6
63	To indicate the duration of an action	说明动作持续的时间	14

序号 / No.	英文 / English	汉语 / Chinese	课次 / Lesson
64	To indicate the options	表达选择	15
65	To indicate when an action will be done	表达什么时间做什么事	5
66	To show modesty	表达谦虚	14
67	To show the way	指路	11
68	To introduce the number of family members	介绍家庭成员数量	3
69	To make a proposal and hope the other party to agree	提出建议并希望同意	15
70	To order food	点菜	10
71	To praise someone	表达称赞	14
72	To relate something as told by another	表达转述	8
73	To relate something as told by another	表达转述	12
74	To respond to thanks	回复感谢	4
75	To say goodbye	告别	1
76	To talk about the weather	谈论天气	12
77	The abbreviated form of asking the other person the same question	询问对方相同问题的简略形式	3
78	The way to read RMB	人民币的读法	9
79	The way to read the time	钟点的读法	5

习写字总表 Table of characters to be learned to write

课号 Lesson	生字 Character	英译 English
1	你	you
	好	good, fine
	什	what
	么	*a suffix*
	名	name
	字	(Chinese) character
	我	I, me
	叫	to be called
	老	*a prefix*
	师	teacher
	再	again
	见	to see
2	是	to be
	哪	which
	国	nation, country
	人	person, people
	中	middle, center
	吗	*used at the end of an interrogative sentence*
	学	to study, to learn
	生	student
	也	too, also
	不	no, not
	她	she, her
	谁	who

课号 Lesson	生字 Character	英译 English
3	家	family
	有	to have
	几	how many
	口	*measure word for family members*
	爸	father
	妈	mother
	妹	younger sister
	哥	elder brother
	和	and
	呢	*used at the end of an interrogative sentence*
	爱	to love
	没	to not have
	一	one
	二	two
	三	three
	四	four
	五	five
	六	six
	七	seven
	八	eight
	九	nine
	十	ten
	两	two

课号 Lesson	生字 Character	英译 English
4	请	please
	问	to ask
	在	to be in/on/at
	儿	*a suffix*
	那	that
	这	this
	汉	Chinese
	语	language
	怎	how
	说	to say
	客	guest
	气	manner, bearing
5	现	now
	点	o'clock
	半	half
	吃	to eat, to have
	午	noon
	饭	meal
	每	every
	早	morning; early
	上	to be engaged (in work, study, etc.) at a fixed time
	下	to be off (work, school, etc.)
	课	class
	晚	evening; late
	睡	to sleep
	觉	sleep

课号 Lesson	生字 Character	英译 English
6	今	present
	天	day
	星	star
	期	period
	月	month
	号	date
	明	immediately following this year or this day, next
	很	very
	高	high
	兴	excitement
	周	week
	末	end
	愉	pleased, happy
	快	pleased, happy
7	打	to play (ball games, etc.)
	篮	basket
	球	ball
	喜	to like
	欢	joyous
	听	to listen
	看	to watch
	音	sound
	乐	music
	网	(the) Internet
	玩	to play
	电	electricity
	脑	brain
	影	shadow

课号 Lesson	生字 Character	英译 English
8	舒	easy, leisurely
	服	to be accustomed to
	肚	stomach, belly
	子	*a suffix*
	疼	painful
	拉	to defecate
	能	can
	来	to come
	累	tired
	想	to want
	休	to rest
	息	to stop
9	您	(*formal, honorific*) you
	买	to buy
	卖	to sell
	水	water
	果	fruit
	钱	money
	多	many, much, more
	少	few, little, less
	要	to want
	共	total
	了	*used after a verb or an adjective to indicate the completion of an actual or expected action or a change*
	花	to spend

课号 Lesson	生字 Character	英译 English
10	包	package
	份	portion, serving
	西	west
	红	red
	鸡	chicken
	蛋	egg
	瓶	bottle
	可	can, may
	乐	happy, glad
	碗	bowl
	米	rice
	菜	food, dish
11	去	to go
	地	ground
	铁	iron; railway
	往	to, towards
	前	front, ahead
	走	to walk
	到	to arrive, to reach
	以	with, by
	坐	to sit
	半	half
	小	small
	时	time
	打	to take (a taxi)
	车	vehicle

课号 Lesson	生字 Character	英译 English
12	错	wrong, bad
	冷	cold
	热	hot
	的	*a particle*
	昨	yesterday
	太	too, extremely
	怎	why, how
	么	*a suffix*
	样	appearance
	会	can, might
	雨	rain
13	红	red
	绿	green
	白	white
	黑	black
	蓝	blue
	颜	color
	色	color
	真	really
	漂	*a bound morpheme*
	亮	bright, light
	还	still
	衬	to put a lining inside sth.
	衫	unlined upper garment
	裤	trousers, pants

课号 Lesson	生字 Character	英译 English
14	长	long
	年	year
	觉	to feel
	得	*a particle*
	难	difficult
	声	voice, sound
	调	tone
	里	in, inside
	马	horse
	虎	tiger
	写	to write
	唱	to sing
	歌	song
15	回	to go back
	告	to tell
	诉	to tell
	邮	to mail
	箱	box
	手	hand
	机	machine
	码	code
	短	short
	信	letter, nessage
	微	tiny, little
	路	road
	平	peaceful, quiet
	安	safe

生词总表 Vocabulary

序号 No.	英文 English translation	生词 Word	拼音 *Pinyin*	词类 Part(s) of speech	课次 Lesson
A					
1	a little	一点儿	yìdiǎnr	num.-cl.	14
2	a modest expression usually used after being praised	哪里	nǎli	pron.	14
3	**a modest expression usually used after being praised**	马马虎虎	mǎmǎhūhū	adj.	14
4	a particle indicating possession or modification	的	de	part.	6
5	afternoon	下午	xiàwǔ	n.	5
6	again	再	zài	adv.	1
7	altogether, in total	一共	yígòng	adv.	9
8	American	美国人	měiguórén		2
9	and	和	hé	conj.	3
10	apple	苹果	píngguǒ	n.	9
B					
11	ball	球	qiú	n.	7
12	basket	篮	lán	n.	7
13	basketball	篮球	lánqiú	n.	7
14	beautiful, good-looking	好看	hǎokàn	adj.	14
15	beautiful, pretty	漂亮	piàoliang	adj.	13
16	bed	床	chuáng	n.	5
17	birthday	生日	shēngrì	n.	6
18	black	黑	hēi	adj.	13
19	black	黑色	hēisè	n.	13
20	blue	蓝	lán	adj.	13
21	bottle	瓶	píng	n.	10
22	bowl	碗	wǎn	n.	10

序号 No.	英文 English translation	生词 Word	拼音 Pinyin	词类 Part(s) of speech	课次 Lesson
23	box	箱	xiāng	n.	15
24	breakfast	早饭	zǎofàn	n.	5
25	bus	公交车	gōngjiāochē	n.	11
C					
26	can	能	néng	v.	8
27	can, may	可以	kěyǐ	v.	11
28	can, might	会	huì	v.	12
29	can, to be able to	会	huì	v.	14
30	chicken	鸡	jī	n.	10
31	(Chinese) character	字	zì	n.	1
32	Chinese (language)	汉语	Hànyǔ	p.n.	4
33	Chinese character	汉字	Hànzì	p.n.	14
34	Chinese food	中国菜	zhōngguócài		10
35	Chinese language	中文	Zhōngwén	p.n.	14
36	Chinese song	中文歌	zhōngwéngē		14
37	Chinese	汉	Hàn		4
38	class	课	kè	n.	5
39	classroom	教室	jiàoshì	n.	4
40	(cooked) rice	米饭	mǐfàn	n.	10
41	Coke	可乐	kělè	n.	10
42	cold	冷	lěng	adj.	12
43	college student	大学生	dàxuéshēng	n.	2
44	college, university	大学	dàxué	n.	2
45	color	色	sè		13
46	color	颜色	yánsè	n.	13
47	comfortable	舒服	shūfu	adj.	8
48	computer	电脑	diànnǎo	n.	7
49	cowboy	牛仔	niúzǎi	n.	13

序号 No.	英文 English translation	生词 Word	拼音 Pinyin	词类 Part(s) of speech	课次 Lesson
D					
50	date	号	hào	m.	6
51	day	日	rì		6
52	day	天	tiān	m.	5
53	delicious	好吃	hǎochī	adj.	10
54	difficult	难	nán	adj.	14
55	dinner, supper	晚饭	wǎnfàn	n.	5
56	(duration of) time	时候	shíhou	n.	15
57	dumpling	饺子	jiǎozi	n.	10
E					
58	egg	蛋	dàn	n.	10
59	egg	鸡蛋	jīdàn	n.	10
60	elder brother	哥哥	gēge	n.	3
61	elder sister	姐姐	jiějie	n.	3
62	email address	邮箱	yóuxiāng	n.	15
63	end	末	mò	n.	6
64	evening, night	晚上	wǎnshang	n.	5
65	evening; late	晚	wǎn	n.	5
66	every day	每天	měi tiān		5
67	every	每	měi	pron.	5
68	excuse me	请问	qǐngwèn	v.	4
F					
69	family	家	jiā	n.	3
70	father	爸爸	bàba	n.	3
71	(*formal, honorific*) you	您	nín	pron.	9
72	food, dish	菜	cài	n.	10
73	for, to	给	gěi	prep.	15
74	four	四	sì	num.	3
75	front, ahead	前	qián	n.	11

序号 No.	英文 English translation	生词 Word	拼音 Pinyin	词类 Part(s) of speech	课次 Lesson
76	fruit	水果	shuǐguǒ	n.	9
G					
77	game	游戏	yóuxì	n.	7
78	glad, happy	高兴	gāoxìng	adj.	6
79	good, fine	好	hǎo	adj.	1
80	good, not bad	不错	búcuò	adj.	12
81	goodbye, bye-bye	再见	zàijiàn	v.	1
82	green	绿	lǜ	adj.	13
83	green	绿色	lǜsè	n.	13
H					
84	half	半	bàn	num.	5
85	hand	手	shǒu	n.	15
86	here	这儿	zhèr	pron.	4
87	hobby	爱好	àihào	n.	7
88	hot	热	rè	adj.	12
89	hour	小时	xiǎoshí	n.	11
90	how about	怎么样	zěnmeyàng	pron.	12
91	how long	多长	duō cháng		14
92	how many	几	jǐ	pron.	3
93	how many, how much	多少	duōshao	pron.	9
94	how	怎么	zěnme	pron.	4
95	hygiene; sanitary	卫生	wèishēng	n./adj.	4
I					
96	I, me	我	wǒ	pron.	1
97	immediately following this year or this day, next	明	míng		6
98	*indicating a plural form*	们	men	suf.	1
J					
99	Japan	日本	Rìběn	p.n.	2

序号 No.	英文 English translation	生词 Word	拼音 Pinyin	词类 Part(s) of speech	课次 Lesson
100	Japanese	日本人	rìběnrén		2
101	jeans	牛仔裤	niúzǎikù	n.	13
102	journey	一路	yílù	n.	15
103	just, only	就	jiù	adv.	11
K					
104	*kuai,* the colloquial form of *yuan,* the basic unit of money in China	块	kuài	m.	9
L					
105	language	语	yǔ		4
106	letter, message	信	xìn	n.	15
107	long	长	cháng	adj.	14
108	lunch	午饭	wǔfàn	n.	5
M					
109	machine	机	jī		15
110	mail	邮件	yóujiàn	n.	15
111	many, much, more	多	duō	adj.	9
112	*mao,* a fractional unit of money in China, ten cents	毛	máo	m.	9
113	meal	饭	fàn	n.	5
114	meaning	意思	yìsi	n.	4
115	meaning, interest	意思	yìsi	n.	14
116	*measure word for family members*	口	kǒu	m.	3
117	message, text message	短信	duǎnxìn	n.	15
118	Mexican	墨西哥人	mòxīgērén		2
119	Mexico	墨西哥	Mòxīgē	p.n.	2
120	middle school student	中学生	zhōngxuéshēng	n.	2
121	middle school	中学	zhōngxué	n.	2
122	minute	分钟	fēnzhōng	n.	11
123	mobile phone	手机	shǒujī	n.	15
124	money	钱	qián	n.	9

序号 No.	英文 English translation	生词 Word	拼音 Pinyin	词类 Part(s) of speech	课次 Lesson
125	month	月	yuè	n.	6
126	morning	上午	shàngwǔ	n.	5
127	morning	早上	zǎoshang	n.	5
128	*most commonly used esp. before nouns which do not have special measure words of their own*	个	gè	m.	3
129	mother	妈妈	māma	n.	3
130	movie	电影	diànyǐng	n.	7
131	music	音乐	yīnyuè	n.	7
N					
132	name	名	míng	n.	1
133	name	名字	míngzi	n.	1
134	nation, country	国	guó	n.	2
135	need not	不用	búyòng	adv.	11
136	no, not	不	bù	adv.	2
137	noon	午	wǔ		5
138	noon	中午	zhōngwǔ	n.	5
139	now	现在	xiànzài	n.	5
140	number	号码	hàomǎ	n.	15
O					
141	o'clock	点	diǎn	m.	5
142	one	一	yī	num.	3
143	or	还是	háishi	conj.	13
144	or	或者	huòzhě	conj.	15
P					
145	painful	疼	téng	adj.	8
146	person, people	人	rén	n.	2
147	(*plural*) you	你们	nǐmen	pron.	1
148	pleasant to hear	好听	hǎotīng	adj.	14
149	pleasant	愉快	yúkuài	adj.	6

序号 No.	英文 English translation	生词 Word	拼音 Pinyin	词类 Part(s) of speech	课次 Lesson
150	please	请	qǐng	v.	4
151	polite	客气	kèqi	adj./v.	4
152	portion, serving	份	fèn	m.	10
153	present	今	jīn		6
154	public traffic	公交	gōngjiāo	n.	11
Q					
155	quite	挺	tǐng	adv.	14
R					
156	rain	雨	yǔ	n.	12
157	really	真	zhēn	adv.	13
158	red	红	hóng	adj.	13
159	red	红色	hóngsè	n.	13
160	rice	米	mǐ	n.	10
161	room	间	jiān		4
S					
162	safe	平安	píng'ān	adj.	15
163	Saturday	星期六	xīngqīliù	n.	6
164	she, her	她	tā	pron.	2
165	shirt	衬衫	chènshān	n.	13
166	short	短	duǎn	adj.	15
167	song	歌	gē	n.	14
168	South Korea	韩国	Hánguó	p.n.	2
169	South Korean	韩国人	hánguórén		2
170	station	站	zhàn	n.	11
171	steamed stuffed bun	包子	bāozi	n.	10
172	stomach, belly	肚子	dùzi	n.	8
173	student	生	shēng		2
174	subway	地铁	dìtiě	n.	11
175	subway station	地铁站	dìtiězhàn	n.	11

序号 No.	英文 English translation	生词 Word	拼音 Pinyin	词类 Part(s) of speech	课次 Lesson
176	Sunday	星期天	xīngqītiān	n.	6
T					
177	teacher	老师	lǎoshī	n.	1
178	(the) Internet	网	wǎng	n.	7
179	that	那	nà	pron.	10
180	the basic unit of weight in China, equal to 500 grams	斤	jīn	m.	9
181	the Imperial Palace	故宫	Gùgōng	p.n.	11
182	the United States	美国	Měiguó	p.n.	2
183	there	那儿	nàr	pron.	4
184	they, them	他们	tāmen	pron.	3
185	this	这	zhè	pron.	10
186	time	时间	shíjiān	n.	14
187	tired	累	lèi	adj.	8
188	to arrive, to reach	到	dào	v.	11
189	to ask	问	wèn	v.	4
190	to attend class	上课	shàng kè	v.	5
191	to be born	生	shēng	v.	6
192	to be engaged (in work, study, etc.) at a fixed time	上	shàng	v.	5
193	to be in/on/at	在	zài	v.	4
194	to be off (work, school, etc.)	下	xià	v.	5
195	to be	是	shì	v.	2
196	to buy	买	mǎi	v.	9
197	to call, to be known as	叫	jiào	v.	1
198	to come	来	lái	v.	8
199	to eat, to have	吃	chī	v.	5
200	to feel	觉得	juéde	v.	14
201	to finish class	下课	xià kè	v.	5
202	to fry	炒	chǎo	v.	10

序号 No.	英文 English translation	生词 Word	拼音 Pinyin	词类 Part(s) of speech	课次 Lesson
203	to get up	起床	qǐ chuáng	v.	5
204	to go back	回	huí	v.	15
205	to go	去	qù	v.	11
206	to have a safe journey	一路平安	yílù píng'ān		15
207	to have diarrhea	拉肚子	lā dùzi		8
208	to have	有	yǒu	v.	3
209	to hear of	听说	tīngshuō	v.	12
210	to like	喜欢	xǐhuan	v.	7
211	to listen, to hear	听	tīng	v.	7
212	to look	看	kàn	v.	14
213	to love	爱	ài	v.	3
214	to mail	邮	yóu	v.	15
215	to not have	没	méi	v.	3
216	to not have	没有	méiyǒu	v.	3
217	to play	玩儿	wánr	v.	7
218	to play (ball games, etc.)	打	dǎ	v.	7
219	to rain	下雨	xià yǔ		12
220	to rest	休息	xiūxi	v.	8
221	to rise to one's feet	起	qǐ	v.	5
222	to say	说	shuō	v.	4
223	to see	见	jiàn	v.	1
224	to sell	卖	mài	v.	9
225	to send	发	fā	v.	15
226	to sleep	睡觉	shuì jiào	v.	5
227	to spend	花	huā	v.	9
228	to study, to learn	学	xué	v.	14
229	to surf the Internet	上网	shàng wǎng	v.	7
230	to take a taxi	打车	dǎ chē	v.	11
231	to tell	告诉	gàosu	v.	15

序号 No.	英文 English translation	生词 Word	拼音 Pinyin	词类 Part(s) of speech	课次 Lesson
232	to thank	谢谢	xièxie	v.	4
233	to walk	走	zǒu	v.	11
234	to want	想	xiǎng	v.	8
235	to want	要	yào	v.	9
236	to watch	看	kàn	v.	7
237	to wear	穿	chuān	v.	13
238	to write	写	xiě	v.	14
239	to, towards	往	wǎng	prep.	11
240	today	今天	jīntiān	n.	6
241	toilet, restroom	卫生间	wèishēngjiān	n.	4
242	tomato	西红柿	xīhóngshì	n.	10
243	tomorrow	明天	míngtiān	n.	6
244	tone	调	diào	n.	14
245	tone	声调	shēngdiào	n.	14
246	too, also	也	yě	adv.	2
247	too, extremely	太……了	tài…le		12
248	trousers, pants	裤	kù		13
249	T-shirt	T恤	T xù		13
U					
250	used after a verb or an adjective to indicate the completion of an actual or expected action or a change	了	le	part.	9
251	used at the end of a sentence to indicate the completion of an action or a change	了	le	part.	8
252	used at the end of an interrogative sentence	呢	ne	part.	3
253	used at the end of an interrogative sentence	吗	ma	part.	2
254	(usually used before measure words and before 半，千，万，and 亿) two	两	liǎng	num.	3

序号 No.	英文 English translation	生词 Word	拼音 Pinyin	词类 Part(s) of speech	课次 Lesson
V					
255	vehicle	车	chē	n.	11
256	very	很	hěn	adv.	6
257	voice, sound	声	shēng	n.	14
W					
258	weather	天气	tiānqì	n.	12
259	WeChat	微信	wēixìn	n.	15
260	week	星期	xīngqī	n.	6
261	week	周	zhōu	n.	6
262	weekend	周末	zhōumò	n.	6
263	what	什么	shénme	pron.	1
264	what, how	多	duō	pron.	14
265	where	哪儿	nǎr	pron.	4
266	which	哪	nǎ	pron.	2
267	white	白	bái	adj.	13
268	white	白色	báisè	n.	13
269	who	谁	shéi	pron.	2
270	will	要	yào	v.	15
271	wrong, bad	错	cuò	adj.	12
Y					
272	yes	是的	shì de		2
273	yesterday	昨天	zuótiān	n.	12
274	You are welcome.	不客气	bú kèqi		4
275	you	你	nǐ	pron.	1
276	younger brother	弟弟	dìdi	n.	3
277	younger sister	妹妹	mèimei	n.	3
278	*yuan*, the basic unit of money in China	元	yuán	m.	9

补充词语总表 Supplementary words

序号 No.	英文 English translation	生词 Word	拼音 Pinyin	词类 Part(s) of speech	课次 Lesson
A					
1	airport	机场	jīchǎng	n.	11
2	although	虽然	suīrán	conj.	14
3	autumn	秋天	qiūtiān	n.	12
B					
4	back	后	hòu	n.	11
5	banana	香蕉	xiāngjiāo	n.	9
6	beverage	饮料	yǐnliào	n.	10
7	big, heavy (rain, etc)	大	dà	adj.	12
8	book	书	shū	n.	7
9	but	但是	dànshì	conj.	14
C					
10	cat	猫	māo	n.	3
11	China	中国	Zhōngguó	p.n.	2
12	chopstick(s)	筷子	kuàizi	n.	10
13	clothes	衣服	yīfu	n.	13
14	cloud	云	yún	n.	12
15	cloudy	多云	duōyún	n.	12
16	cool	凉快	liángkuai	adj.	12
D					
17	degree (of intensity, hardness, heat, etc.)	度	dù	num.	12
18	doctor	医生	yīshēng	n.	8
19	dog	狗	gǒu	n.	3
20	dormitory	宿舍	sùshè	n.	4
E					
21	elementary school student, pupil	小学生	xiǎoxuéshēng	n.	2

序号 No.	英文 English translation	生词 Word	拼音 Pinyin	词类 Part(s) of speech	课次 Lesson
22	English	英语	Yīngyǔ	p.n.	4
F					
23	foot	足	zú	n.	7
24	football	足球	zúqiú	n.	7
25	France	法国	Fǎguó	p.n.	2
26	French	法语	Fǎyǔ	p.n.	4
G					
27	Good evening!	晚上好	wǎnshang hǎo		1
28	Good morning!	早上好	zǎoshang hǎo		1
29	grape	葡萄	pútao	n.	9
30	gray	灰	huī	adj.	13
H					
31	hat	帽子	màozi	n.	13
32	head	头	tóu	n.	8
33	heavy rain	大雨	dàyǔ	n.	12
I					
34	ice water	冰水	bīng shuǐ		10
J					
35	Japanese	日语	Rìyǔ	p.n.	4
K					
36	Korean	韩语	Hányǔ	p.n.	4
L					
37	left	左	zuǒ	n.	11
38	library	图书馆	túshūguǎn	n.	11
39	light rain	小雨	xiǎoyǔ	n.	12
M					
40	(maternal) grandma	外婆	wàipó	n.	3
41	(maternal) grandpa	外公	wàigōng	n.	3
42	mango	芒果	mángguǒ	n.	9

序号 No.	英文 English translation	生词 Word	拼音 Pinyin	词类 Part(s) of speech	课次 Lesson
N					
43	noodle(s)	面条儿	miàntiáor	n.	10
O					
44	orange	橙子	chéngzi	n.	9
45	overcast	阴	yīn	adj.	12
P					
46	(paternal) grandma	奶奶	nǎinai	n.	3
47	(paternal) grandpa	爷爷	yéye	n.	3
48	pair (*used for shoes, socks, etc.*)	双	shuāng	m.	13
49	pair, piece (*used for pants, skirts, etc.*)	条	tiáo	m.	13
50	pear	梨	lí	n.	9
51	piece (*used for clothes*)	件	jiàn	m.	13
52	plate	盘	pán	m.	10
R					
53	restaurant	饭馆	fànguǎn	n.	11
54	right	右	yòu	n.	11
55	Russia	俄罗斯	Éluósī	p.n.	2
56	Russian	俄语	Éyǔ	p.n.	4
S					
57	shorts	短裤	duǎnkù	n.	13
58	small	小	xiǎo	adj.	12
59	snow	雪	xuě	n.	12
60	socks	袜子	wàzi	n.	13
61	Spain	西班牙	Xībānyá	p.n.	2
62	Spanish	西班牙语	Xībānyáyǔ	p.n.	4
63	spring	春天	chūntiān	n.	12
64	summer	夏天	xiàtiān	n.	12
65	sun	太阳	tàiyang	n.	12

序号 No.	英文 English translation	生词 Word	拼音 Pinyin	词类 Part(s) of speech	课次 Lesson
66	sunny	晴	qíng	adj.	12
67	supermarket	超市	chāoshì	n.	4
T					
68	table tennis	乒乓球	pīngpāngqiú	n.	7
69	telephone	电话	diànhuà	n.	15
70	tennis	网球	wǎngqiú	n.	7
71	throat	嗓子	sǎngzi	n.	8
72	to ask for leave	请假	qǐng jià	v.	8
73	to be windy	刮风	guā fēng		12
74	to cough	咳嗽	késou	v.	8
75	to do sports; sport	运动	yùndòng	v./n.	7
76	to drink	喝	hē	v.	10
77	to get ill	生病	shēng bìng	v.	8
78	to have a cold; cold	感冒	gǎnmào	v./n.	8
79	to have a fever	发烧	fā shāo	v.	8
80	to hope, to wish	希望	xīwàng	v.	15
81	to phone sb.	打电话	dǎ diànhuà		15
82	to play football	踢足球	tī zúqiú		7
83	to play table tennis	打乒乓球	dǎ pīngpāngqiú		7
84	to play tennis	打网球	dǎ wǎngqiú		7
85	to practice *taijiquan*	打太极拳	dǎ tàijíquán		7
86	to read	读	dú	v.	4
87	to read a book	看书	kàn shū		7
88	to sing	唱歌	chàng gē	v.	7
89	to snow	下雪	xià xuě		12
90	to walk	走路	zǒu lù	v.	11
91	to watch TV	看电视	kàn diànshì		7
92	to welcome	欢迎	huānyíng	v.	15

序号 No.	英文 English translation	生词 Word	拼音 *Pinyin*	词类 Part(s) of speech	课次 Lesson
93	to write a letter	写信	xiě xìn		15
94	trousers, pants	裤子	kùzi	n.	13
95	TV	电视	diànshì	n.	7
W					
96	UK	英国	Yīngguó	p.n.	2
W					
97	warm	暖和	nuǎnhuo	adj.	12
98	WeChat Moments, an app function	朋友圈	péngyouquān		15
99	wind	风	fēng	n.	12
100	winter	冬天	dōngtiān	n.	12
Y					
101	yellow	黄	huáng	adj.	13